BARBARIANS

A HANDBOOK FOR ASPIRING SAVAGES

BARBARIANS
A HANDBOOK FOR ASPIRING SAVAGES

BY DR. BYRON CLAVICLE
and GRÜTE SKULLBASHER

With contributions by BENJAMIN CHADWICK

illustrated by JOSHUA KEMBLE

INSIGHT EDITIONS

San Rafael, CA

INSIGHT EDITIONS

PO Box 3088
San Rafael, CA 94912
www.insighteditions.com

Text copyright © 2011 by Benjamin Chadwick
Illustrations copyright © 2011 by Joshua Kemble

Library of Congress Cataloging-in-Publication Data available.

ISBN: 978-1-60887-024-0

 ✹ Replanted Paper

Insight Editions, in association with Roots of Peace, will plant two trees for each tree used in the manufacturing of this book. Roots of Peace is an internationally renowned humanitarian organization dedicated to eradicating land mines worldwide and converting war-torn lands into productive farms and wildlife habitats. Together, we will plant two million fruit and nut trees in Afghanistan and provide farmers there with the skills and support necessary for sustainable land use.

Printed in the USA by Insight Editions

10 9 8 7 6 5 4 3 2 1

CONTENTS

5 BARBARIAN ACCOMPLISHMENTS

6 BARBARIANS AND MODERN LIFE

APPENDICES

NOTES FROM THE AUTHORS

Dear ladies, gentlemen, and other readers,

This book represents the culmination of a detailed study of barbarians, researched during a period wherein my erstwhile nemesis, Grüte Skullbasher, imprisoned me in the mightiest tower of his kingdom in Passaic, New Jersey. I passed the time during my captivity etching these collected documents on my own skin using fragments of bone from former prisoners and presented the original manuscript bound with lengths of my own hair and snot. Thankfully, Insight Editions accorded me the honor of publishing this compilation of my anthropological notes, under the condition that I soak the entire text in hydrogen peroxide before delivery and then laminate and scrub it a second time.

I believe, and hope the following study will confirm, that I am one of the world's foremost experts on barbarian anthropology. Nevertheless, none of this would have been possible without the advice of, and beatings from, Grüte Skullbasher. Through the undeniable force of his existence, Grüte has contributed vastly to my own, and academia's—nay, humankind's—understanding of barbarian culture. Such a degree of knowledge was, until now, available only to readers of advertisements found in the back pages of pornographic wrestling magazines.

I'd also like to thank my assistant, Benjamin Chadwick, who transcribed and then assembled my assorted notes into a more-or-less readable condition. Benjamin also provided other valuable input and support when I was nearly squashed by crushing deadlines and clubs with rusty nails sticking out of them when I tried to convince Grüte that Vivaldi is better than Van Halen.

As a condition of his assistance, for which I am most grateful, Grüte was presented with a case of Pabst Blue Ribbon, a ticket for All-You-Can-Eat Yak Ribs Night at Benihana, and an honorary doctorate from Princeton. Mr. Chadwick was provided with blows to the head and a bus ticket back to his home in a Tijuana trailer park.

In these pages you will find several monographs of my research supplemented, in some cases, by the words of Dr. Skullbasher. In some places I have paraphrased Grüte into serviceable English, but most of his quotes have been provided verbatim.

In closing, I would like to once again thank Insight Editions, Venice Beach University, Mr. Chadwick, and Dr. Skullbasher.

Yours in traction,

Dr. Byron Clavicle

Dr. Byron Clavicle, PhD, DDS, PCP, and LMNOP
The Marc Singer Distinguished Chairman of
* Barbarian-American Studies*
Barbarian Studies Department
Venice Beach University

DEAR PATHETIC MAGGOTS,

UGHHHH. NYARGGHHH. GRAWWRGG!

YOURS IN CONQUEST,

HIS HOLY EMINENCE DR. GRÜTE SKULLBASHER
DEAN OF DISCIPLINE
PRINCETON UNIVERSITY

SCHOLARLY FOUNDATIONS

UNDERSTANDING BARBARIAN SCHOLARSHIP

Before I continue, it is important to note one essential fact about barbarian scholarship. Because barbarians are mostly illiterate, there exist very few of the written and material records historians typically analyze when researching an ancient culture. Undaunted by such a challenge, I have based my scholarship in this book on an amalgam of disparate sources, such as:

- what little does exist of a barbarian archaeological record (mostly crude weaponry and bones).
- written accounts of barbarians from their civilized neighbors, such as the Romans and Canadians.
- the trailblazing scholarship of Robert E. Howard, who fictionalized his findings in his tales of Kull and Conan.
- visionary cinematic masterpieces depicting barbarian life, such as *Ator, the Fighting Eagle* (1982).
- interactions with and observations of barbarians living their lifestyle in contemporary society (for example, Grüte Skullbasher).

Where the record was too spotty to make accurate academic assertions, which was at least 95 percent of the time, I have simply made shit up and called it fact.

As a consequence of this unorthodox academic methodology, there are three distinct periods of barbarianism jumbled together in these pages:

1 – barbarians of prehistory (mostly from the Hyborian Age) and outer space
2 – historical barbarians, malingerers at the fringes of civilization, not unlike teenagers lurking outside a Drug Free School Zone
3 – modern barbarians, who can be spotted on ESPN2 and pigging out at Popeyes when there's a special offer on popcorn chicken

GRÜTE SAYS

To the hell fires with "sources"! By will of Crom, I break your glasses!

WHAT IS A BARBARIAN?

To answer this question, it is best first to describe what a barbarian is not. A barbarian is not a model of automobile, a hair-restoration drug, or a cello. Nor is a barbarian something you can order online (unless you live in Hawaii or Alaska). A barbarian cannot be used as a taxi or to scrape barnacles off a boat. Notable contemporary nonbarbarians include Helen Mirren, Wallace Shawn, Kelsey Grammer, and Marilu Henner.

The word "barbarian" comes from the Greek *barbaros*, meaning "foreign," but in modern parlance it is shorthand for a very specific type of individual or existence. By the modern definition, a barbarian lives outside the borders of the dominant, effeminate, lazy, weak culture that scientists refer to as civilization. Barbarians are distinguished by their fundamental irreverence—not in the comedic sense, mind you, but in their complete and total disregard for the social rules we civilized people take for granted. Consider the supermarket and the everyday practice of grocery shopping. A civilized person can be found gathering products and then patiently standing in the checkout line to exit. A barbarian can be found in the meat department, tearing into the packages of raw meat—gorging on animal flesh, Styrofoam, and plastic—and then ripping off the arms of the butcher and eating those, too.

As barbarians are quite deadly, it is difficult to observe them for any length of time. Scholarly studies, though, have documented that a barbarian can be identified according to four main characteristics: physique, clothing, diction, and the etymology of his or her name. Let us review each characteristic in detail:

PHYSIQUE: There are very few scrawny barbarians. If you see individuals with biceps bigger than their craniums, chances are they are at least half-barbarian. To get such a physique, they must lift heavy things, conquer civilizations, and eat a lot of protein. Categorically, there are no vegetarian barbarians (this notion is an oxymoron) and the two tribes (vegetarians and barbarians) frequently war with each other, except on the neutral ground of Renaissance faires. Generally, barbarians see vegetables as food for animals, enemies, and slaves.

CLOTHING: Barbarians usually wear codpieces, loincloths, or goatskin Speedos. For this reason, they are often mistaken for professional wrestlers. In colder weather—for example, when galloping on horseback across the moonlit Asiatic steppe—barbarians will at least throw a dead animal over their shoulders, or sprout prodigious back hair. Studded black leather was common until recently, but has fallen out of fashion except among barbarian leather daddies. The animal skins used for supplementary bits of clothing can help identify the tribe. In Europe, deerskins and bearskins are common; in Africa, barbarians wear the hides of tigers and apes. In the Pacific Northwest, local barbarians wear jackets made from spotted owls or vampires.

DICTION: Barbarians are taciturn by nature. They rarely have a large vocabulary. In fact, they rarely have a vocabulary at all. But they are not soft spoken. There is indeed nothing about a barbarian that is soft, except after a good meal or sex.

One will never find a barbarian named Percival or Thurman. On the Yor Scale, which measures name masculinity, a barbarian's proper name will rate at least a 7 (see the table below). A full barbarian name is usually Something the Something-or-other (see Appendix D, "How to Make a Barbarian Movie," page 158, for more information on barbarian naming conventions). A female barbarian name is always suffixed with -na or -ra, as in She-Ra, Sheena, or Tyra. There are exceptions, of course, but they merely serve to prove the rule.

MAJOR BARBARIAN CLASSIFICATIONS

The Diagnostic and Statistical Barbarian Classification Directory (abbreviated as the DSBCD and quickly forgotten) lists two major orders of barbarians: high-functioning and low-functioning. Anthropologists have analyzed extensive notes from field observations and conducted carefully controlled experiments to measure the differences between the two.

As a rule, high-functioning barbarians (HFBs) are somewhat technologically advanced. Their societies include a catalog of basic infrastructure. For starters, they have knowledge of irrigation, mining, and roads. They also have a spoken

THE YOR SCALE OF NAME MASCULINITY

0 (lowest)—Sue	6 Mack, Spike, Clem
1 Percy, Skippy, Patty	7 Big Mack, Killer, Mutton-Chop
2 Cubby, Kippie, Nicky	8 Tor, Caliban, Aëdwulf, Hawk
3 Lawrence, Delfeayo, Antoine	9 Kungôr, Thundarr, Hagbard
4 Norman, Donovan, Franz	10 (highest)—Grüte
5 Steve, Tommy, Joe, Fergus	

language, some degree of metallurgy, a material culture, religion and philosophy, a sense of geography and accompanying practices for navigation, and so on.

Low-functioning barbarians (LFBs), on the other hand, are essentially screaming hordes that wave heavy clubs in the air as they descend upon your peaceful way of life, raise hell, and run off with your daughters slung over their shoulders. Although HFBs and LFBs seem drastically different on the surface, the two types have more in common than might initially be apparent.

Though worldly by savage standards, HFBs should not be mistaken for civilized people. Being barbaric, they have an upper limit of knowledge. For example, HFBs are incapable of the sustained attention required for reading. In the experiments conducted for the DSBCD, they showed no interest in books with words, but they lingered slightly longer on *Hägar the Horrible* cartoons before setting them aflame. The HFBs fared better at the cinema, cheering during the ultraviolent rapes and beatings in *A Clockwork Orange* (1971) and sleeping through the second half. They absolutely loved *America's Funniest Home Videos* (1990), in particular the clips that feature singing dogs and people injuring themselves with tennis rackets and propane grills. HFBs are easily mistaken for hockey fans: Both are competent enough to buy game tickets and order beers, but otherwise only barely capable of functioning within normal human society.

LFBs make HFBs look like opera buffs. At the experimental screening of *A Clockwork Orange*, the group of LFBs in the audience beat the ushers and raped the control group. By the time the movie ended, the LFBs had already vacated the theater to pillage the nearby food court and dance around a pile of burning Chevrolets in the parking garage. By sunset, the entire mall had been razed and all the women were missing. Two of the anthropologists conducting the study were found several days later severely beaten and tied to the Tree of Woe in the Universal Studios parking lot.

To the extent that LFBs have a value system, it can be summed up with the cliché, "The strong survive." It is common among LFB tribes to slaughter weaker "girly" boys by age thirteen and sacrifice girls who have not sexually matured by age eleven. Among anthropologists, this process is known as "the weedening." Here I should note that Grüte Skullbasher comes from the Bunglorian tribe, which is universally shunned as the most low-functioning of all low-functioning barbarian societies.

HFBs, on the other hand, are not so predisposed to slaughtering their own young. Their talent for basic agriculture and slavery make it easier for them to

SUMMARY OF THE DSBCD BARBARIAN CLASSIFICATION SYSTEM

HIGH-FUNCTIONING BARBARIANS (HFB)

- They have somewhat sophisticated technology.
- They might secretly want to be seen as civilized, or pretend to be.
- They can communicate, at least verbally, although they don't have anything terribly interesting to say.
- Celebrities who might be HFBs: Brigitte Nielsen, Wilt Chamberlain, Ernest Hemingway, Menahem Golan, Yoram Globus, Klaus Kinski, Kevin Sorbo, Cher

LOW-FUNCTIONING BARBARIANS (LFB)

- Their societies are primarily concerned with strength, fighting, decapitation, and rape.
- They like to eat a lot.
- They like to stroke goats.
- Their near-universal illiteracy does not stop them from commenting on YouTube videos.
- Celebrities who might be LFBs: Donald "Ogre" Gibb, Andre the Giant, Ryan Seacrest, Michael Berryman, Richard Kiel, Mike Ditka, Antonin Scalia, Darryl Hannah, Keith Moon, Lindsay Lohan, Bret Easton Ellis, Alexander Ovechkin, Jack Nicholson, Michael Phelps, Madonna

provide for even the most parasitic members of their tribe. In the modern era, they've found employment as mall Santas (shorter HFBs make excellent elves) and as bouncers. HFBs also excel at zymurgy, because it's the only thing they ever found worth learning.

Although not officially sanctioned by the DSBCD, there is also a third category of barbarian society: the matriarchal. Feminist barbarian studies scholars say that this classification has not been recognized by the DSBCD because of the patriarchal assumptions at the core of barbarian studies scholarship, but the truth is that there is only a small number of barbarian societies ruled by women, making it very difficult to observe them and record their defining characteristics. Judging by the limited scholarship available, these societies are just like the patriarchal, only way hotter. In matriarchal LFB societies, such as the Amazons, Californians, and Scythians, for instance, the men's and women's gender roles are reversed, with women leading the hunt, scheduling the goat-stroking, and repeatedly raping the men.

This is in stark contrast to the myth that all women in matriarchal barbarian societies have zero interest in men. Barbarian women who do lack interest in men are known as lesbarbarians, and indeed have been known to congregate in tribes. The misapprehension that all matriarchal barbarian societies are lesbarbarian cultures is likely due to the popularity of the Lesbarsploitation movie genre.

Naturally, there are also gay male barbarians, known colloquially as brokeback barbarians. Hetero barbarian males are surprisingly accepting of their homosexual counterparts, thanks to barbarians' generally libertarian value system and their excessive demand for hairstylists. It is most likely due to such integration that there is little record of brokeback barbarians attempting to construct a common society of their own, despite their inability to quit one another. Such a record is hinted at only in a handful of documentary short films by Andy Warhol and in the imaginings of Annie Proulx. A barbarian who enjoys sex with both women and men is known as a bibarian.

A SAMPLING OF BARBARIAN TRIBES

AMAZONS, CALIFORNIANS, AND SCYTHIANS

All of these are matriarchal tribes, although the similarities end there. The Amazons lived in northern Europe, and the Scythians by the Black Sea. The Californians resided on the ancient island of California, not to be confused

with its namesake state on America's West Coast. Their leader, Califia, led an army of women and griffins against Constantinople and lost, so she converted to Christianity. The griffins chose instead to convert to Judaism. These tribes differ from the matriarchal tribes depicted in the historical drama *Barbarian Queen* (1985) in that they spent much less time putting on makeup. Instead, they were tough, surly warrior women who would bite off your arms if you didn't pay them tribute every February or if you were too lazy to take out the garbage. According to Grüte Skullbasher, these tribes died out because they couldn't find husbands, although I suspect they were happier without them.

AQUILONIANS, BOSSONIANS, BRYTHUNIANS, HYPERBOREANS, HYRKANIANS, NEMEDIANS, SHEMITES, ZINGARANS

These are just some of the diverse peoples who populated our planet during the Hyborian Age. Taken as a collective, they were industrious and militant. If you can follow their complex history, nearly all of them fought each other at one point or another. Over time, most of them merged into modern Bunglorians. Others devolved back into apes. Most of these people worship either Crom or Thoth-Amon (see "Barbarian Religion," page 84). The chief sources for the history of these people are the works of Robert E. Howard, but there are errors in even his scholarship. For example, he declines to mention anywhere in his work that Hyborian Age barbarians had octopus tentacles instead of arms. See also Bunglorians, Cimmerians, and Stygians in this chapter.

ATARIANS

The Atarians were an unusual, heavily magical race that vanished in the mid-1990s, taking much of their history with them. They dwelled inside large, ornate wooden cabinets known as Atarian interdimensional portals. In exchange for small coins, the Atarians would conjure up hallucinations of their tribal history wherein the visitor could reenact famous episodes of Atarian history using primitive plastic buttons and a magical Stick of Joyfulness. The episodes ranged, broadly, from the mission to recover the golden ax from Death Adder to the epic Atarian conquest of the giant Centipedes.

AUSTRALIANS

All Australians are barbarians. They sacked Rome in 487 CE.

BUNGLORIANS

BUNGLORIANS

The Bunglorians are a refined, well-dressed, ingenious, and sexy group of people who are, in all measures, godlike. Not! Grüte Skullbasher is the king of the Bunglorians, and he made me promise to write something nice. Luckily, Grüte can't read. Descended from various Hyborian nations, it is said that Bunglorians are so stupid that they could be outwitted by a spoon, that they wear live raccoons for shoes, and that they think chocolate comes out of a horse's asshole. Bunglorians have one positive defining characteristic: They are massively strong. On both the physical and mental levels, Bunglorians make Arnold Schwarzenegger look like Albert Einstein. There are about three thousand Bunglorians alive nowadays, mostly near Passaic, New Jersey. They stay near one another because they believe they are the Master Race. Consequently, there's a lot of inbreeding. Incidentally, Grüte is also a Republican (see page 24 for a description of this barbarian tribe). However, like most Bunglorians, he is a convicted sex offender and multiple felon and so has been stripped of his right to vote.

CIMMERIANS

Cimmerians are a Hyborian Age race about which much is known, but little can be repeated (for legal reasons). A certain famous barbarian, who was also a destroyer, and whose name rhymes with Onan, was their most famous

CIMMERIANS

citizen. Of him, the less said, the less I have to consult my lawyer. Cimmerians worship Crom, an all-powerful deity. There were also Cimmerians who lived around the Black Sea between the eighth and sixth centuries BCE. Upon learning they'd stolen the earlier tribe's name, the latter-day Cimmerians changed their tribal name and thus disappeared from the historical record altogether.

DISCATECS

The Discatecs ruled part of northeast Honduras from 12,000 BCE until, oh, somewhere around 1492 CE. They lived fairly peaceful lives full of polyester suits, gold chains, mirror balls, and human sacrifice until they were mercilessly slaughtered by Spanish conquistadors. They left behind great stone cities and late-night dance halls that are now covered in vines, snakes, and carnivorous ferns.

EPOKZI-UPTZI

See "A Modern Stone Age Family," page 50.

ETERNIANS

The Eternian barbarians live on a faraway planet. They are the survivors of a great war that destroyed a once advanced civilization, leaving behind only swords, axes, cloaks, and tight, fuzzy briefs.

DISCATECS

ETERNIANS

HAND PEOPLE

The Hand People were led by their charismatic leader Lothar, who carried a gigantic magical theremin. He used this psychedelic instrument to strike fear in the hearts of folk music fans, making them panic and flee to the suburbs. The Hand People took over Greenwich Village briefly in the mid-1960s and then disappeared, probably slaughtered by the Rolling Stones or the Mongols.

HUNS

Seemingly out of nowhere, the Huns swept across Europe in the fifth century, carving their way straight to the heart of the Roman Empire. Their ferocious leader Attila once bit the head off a cow and spat it in the pope's face. After Attila's death, the Huns disappeared, probably intermixing with another civilization. Personally, I think they hitched a ride on a comet and traveled to Alpha Centauri, but not all historians agree.

MOK

The Mok are a race of giant inarticulate cat-men mutants. In 1980, an animated TV show called *Thundarr the Barbarian* chronicled the adventures of Ookla the Mok and his two human companions (a princess and a suicidal buffoon), permanently cementing him as an epic hero in the eyes of viewers worldwide. The Mok language has never been successfully translated, which has for generations made Mok scholarship consistently challenging. The language seems to have evolved from Wookiee, an ancient tongue used in a galaxy far, far away. Moks have a special relationship with equorts (giant bird-horse mutants), which could be symbiotic, parasitic, or possibly sexual. For more about equorts, see "Getting Around," page 36.

MONGOLS

Mongols are undoubtedly the most awesome barbarians in history, from their massive empire and their rampaging, club-wielding hordes to their badass costumes and their unbelievably ass-kicking names like Genghis and Kublai. They came racing out of the Orient and marauded across Europe, leaving nothing but fire, death, and destruction in their wake, ruling everywhere from Cambodia to Chile from around 1200 CE until 1989, when Genghis Khan left the steppes for Hollywood and tried to break into acting in *Bill & Ted's Excellent Adventure* (1989). The only thing the Mongols couldn't do is get over the

MOK

Great Wall of China. Fun fact: When Ronald Reagan famously said, "Mr. Gorbachev, tear down this wall!" he was actually working for the Mongols and pointing at a map of China's northwest border. Of course, it would've been World War III if Gorbachev had tried. But what the hell did Reagan care; he was so senile he thought the White House was on *Sesame Street* and that Nancy was Big Bird.

ORCS

Rising out of the mysterious lands southeast of Middle-Earth, the Orcs were competent fighters notable for their excellent work ethic, lack of conversational finesse, and bad hygiene, much like modern-day software programmers.

PICTS

Despite centuries of scholarship, nobody has any clear idea what a Pict is, even though one sings on the early Pink Floyd album *Ummagumma*.

REPUBLICANS

Industrious, warlike, proudly lacking in artistic culture, bent on plundering the Treasury, incapable of reasoned debate, and determined to destroy civilization, Republicans possess a savagery with which few tribes can compete. It is a safe bet that Republicans will come out on top after their self-inflicted apocalypse. It's never too late to join . . .

GRÜTE SAY!

Give gold to American king to hand out to weak? No! Leech-parasites must be destroyed!

STYGIANS

Stygians are snake-loving freaks from the Hyborian Age, most of whom worship Thoth-Amon. See also Cimmerians, Aquilonians, et al, in this chapter.

REBUBLICANS

VIKINGS

This austere Norse tribe harried Europe throughout the Middle Ages, amphibiously raiding, raping, and pillaging coastal cities in search of animal horns for their ornate helmets. When they had decimated the horn-bearing animals to their satisfaction, the Vikings retired to Minnesota.

VISIGOTHS

"Visigoth" is a Latin word that combines *visi*, meaning "visible," and *goth*, meaning "Goth." They were named this because the normal Goths were so dirty that it was hard to see them when they attacked. By comparison, the Visigoths had quite a distinguished appearance, including ruffled shirts, black capes, white face paint, and black mascara, lipstick, and nail polish. In modern times, they still wear their native dress and can be found in shopping malls and high school drama departments.

VIKINGS

BARBARIAN
BASICS

HOW TO DRESS LIKE A BARBARIAN

Barbarian fashion is about looking good, feeling good, and not letting your clothes get in the way of battle.

FOR MONSIEUR

- There's nothing out there that says, "I'm a barbarian, confident in my sexual identity" quite like a loincloth and matching headband. Choose a brown loincloth that fits snugly in back and reaches halfway down your thigh. Why brown and not a livelier color? Well, brown hides dirt, food residue, dried blood, and just about anything else you might spill on yourself during your conquests. Make sure your loincloth is slit up the sides so you can run. This will also allow you to demurely flash your posterior if you're feeling flirty while scaling a cliff.

- Furry briefs are also popular, and if you choose the right animal pelt you won't even need to shave your bikini zone, since stray hairs will blend in with the fur. Just watch your diet—nothing's more embarrassing than a yak-hair Speedo half hidden by flabby thighs!

- For your headband, keep it simple. Brass or gold. The two sides should meet in the center of your forehead, where they can come together in a simple point, or choose something more decorative, like a skull or a Star of David. Good guys generally don't wear helmets, but if you're feeling naughty, think horns. Or, mix it up with some more elaborate barbarian headgear designs—for some starter ideas, see "Some Awesome Barbarian Hats," page 33.

- Sandals are for pathetic Roman weaklings, so you'll want to invest in a nice pair of boots. Ugg, an Australian company founded by and named for barbarians, has brought these boots back into style, so it's easy to find a pair at your local shopping mall and online. Your boots should match your loincloth or your furry briefs. If you're looking for something a little more robust, sew some woolly mammoth fur to your Uggs, or cut off the legs of a snuffleupagus and wear those.

- Everything beyond these three key pieces of clothing is an accessory. Think straps, straps, straps! Straps across your chest will help lift and separate your massive pectorals. It doesn't matter if they serve no other purpose.

- Leather gauntlets or bracers are helpful sometimes, especially if you dabble in falconry. The talons of a bird of prey can pierce even the toughest bare wrists.

- Accessories should largely be dictated by body type and weapon of choice. If you typically use a sword, you're probably an athletic warrior and might like to use your head in a fight, in which case you absolutely must wear body armor. Bearing in mind that armor has a tendency to cover up your incredible physique, make sure to keep it simple. A golden breastplate is about as far as you can go and still pass for barbaric.

- If, on the other hand, your weapon of choice is a hammer, club, or other blunt instrument, you're probably more of the brawny, bashing type who's carrying around a few extra pounds. Best to cover up some of that flab with a dark, studded leather suit! And don't be afraid to let your body hair do some of the work.

- In winter, of course, you'll want to slip into a dead, furry animal. Any sort of roadkill will do. This year, mange is in.

- And remember, the look isn't complete until you coat yourself in oil.

FOR MADAME

- Before we get started, let's determine your alignment. Do you want to help your local power-mad magician extend his tyrannical empire, steal magical objects, and enslave the peasantry? If that sounds like your kind of thing, you're probably evil. And you're in luck fashionwise, since you have a lot of options. Black leather is the key to your wardrobe. You should make sure to wear a well-oiled, skintight catsuit or a skirt that fits low on the hips, with metal studs, black laces, and reptilian scales.

- If you ally yourself with the good people, your options are a little more limited. Brown leather is definitely the material of choice, but you might mix it up with a chain-mail tank top. Everything about male barbarian loincloths applies equally to barbarians of the fairer sex, except that the length should be quite a bit shorter—quarter-thigh is ideal. Maybe, though, you want to get sassy and go for a minicloth or even a micro-minicloth.

• If you're not sure whether you want to help the wizard or kill him, don't worry. Like 99 percent of barbarians, you have no political opinions of any sort, and that's nothing to be ashamed of. The good news is you can wear whatever you want. Just remember: Men are constantly judging you.

- Whatever your alignment, it would be criminal to hide breasts like yours, even when strutting through snowy tundra. If you're really feeling the cold, throw a cowl or mantle over your back, but don't you dare veil those triple D's. Adventurous European barbaresses have no objection to open bodices or simply topless fashions. Just make sure you won't be doing any running! If you own any magical items that glow, wear them around your neck to draw even more attention to your seismic cleavage. Flash with pride, and pity the so-called civilized people who have to dress down for work.

- You can get a little more ornate with your tiara and gauntlets. Jewelry is, of course, quite welcome, although if you overdo it, you're likely to get attacked more often, and you're already getting attacked every time you go anywhere.

- Instead of wearing your sword and scabbard behind your back, go with a belt. It helps accentuate your hips. *Schwing!*

WOMEN'S SPORTSWEAR: See above.
WOMEN'S SLEEPWEAR: See Women's Sportswear.
WOMEN'S LINGERIE: See Women's Sleepwear.
WOMEN'S WINTER CLOTHING: See Women's Lingerie.

GRÜTE SAYS

Buy extra copy of book and make sexy dolls!

— SOME AWESOME BARBARIAN HATS —

Barbarians have always had excellent taste in hats.

BARBARIAN MAKEOVER!

With your fashion consultant, Grüte Skullbasher

A HAPPY-GO-LUCKY LUMBERJACK

BEFORE:

GRÜTE SAYS

Beard look good, ax look good, but what with stupid shirt? Switch to leather one. Suspenders no good!

AFTER:

GRÜTE SAYS

After makeover, him look almighty!

AN AMBITIOUS POLITICIAN

BEFORE:

GRÜTE SAYS

What wrong with picture? Everything! Woman trying look powerful but source of strength is hidden!

AFTER:

GRÜTE SAYS

Now she look right to conquer world and party all night long!

GETTING AROUND

It's one thing to march a couple of miles to pillage your neighbors or invade an empire's frontier, and quite another to sweep across an entire continent and destroy every village therein. Making your way across mountains and deserts can be daunting. To surmount these challenges, barbarians have employed a variety of transport to cross vast distances in search of food, conquest, booze, and casual rape.

HISTORY

Historically, horses and camels were the most prominent means of transportation, followed by elephants and ponies. But these animals were not always available.

The royal prince of Eternia chose to ride on what seemed like a cowardly tiger. One day, all communication ceased from their capital in Castle Greyskull. After some weeks, a young woman finally ventured inside. All she found were several skeletons and one very fat, lazy tiger.

One lost brand of the Atarian tribe had great luck riding on flying ostriches. Faced with wave after wave of relentless enemy knights on buzzards, though, and the occasional hungry pterodactyl, the warriors' fates were sealed. Their last hope was extinguished when they accidentally flew into a sea of lava.

An Eternian tiger mount

Moks ride on equorts, which are like cute yellow mutant ponies with mohawks, bushy tails, and beaks. Equorts are very accommodating steeds. Unfortunately, they are rare because they taste delicious. Most other steeds don't taste so good.

An equort

TODAY

The barbarian disdain for public transportation is well known. Even literate people find it difficult to decipher bus maps, and barbarians don't have that lexical luxury. Once in a while, though, when shitfaced after fifty-three cans of Glogg, a barbarian will think twice about driving home. In these circumstances they've been known to attempt to board a bus, usually without paying. Urban bus drivers, notoriously intransigent and fearless, are the only people in civilization to regularly stare down barbarians and compel them to fork over a couple bucks for the ride. In moments of tipsy remorse, even a barbarian will sometimes submit to civilization's fatuous logic. They can always restore their self-esteem the following day by sacking the bus station.

When it comes to air travel, most barbarians fly exactly once in their lives—they hate it. At the airport, the security agents always put up a fight about even the smallest broadsword. Once on the plane, the seats are too cramped and there's never enough room in the bathrooms for a standard-size barbarian *and* a stewardess. Those few barbarians who repeat the experience always pay for extra seats and bring their own serving wenches and chamber pot.

72 Camaro Z28

GRÜTE SAYS

Me also like 1972 Camaro Z28 with Rally Sport Option. Big white racing stripe make speedy Camaro go faster! I tore off roof—now it convertible car, fun for cocaine bachelorette party!

COMBAT: A HOW-TO GUIDE

You can learn everything you need to know to fight like a barbarian in just a few simple steps. The most important thing to realize is that enemies never attack in groups: They always engage in combat one at a time.

The lessons that follow work best as part of a montage that summarizes your youth.

SWORD FIGHTING

    1 – Face your opponent.

    2 – Draw swords. Clash swords high.

    3 – Clash swords low.

    4 – Swing and parry.

    5 – Oops. Sword flies off into the bushes.

    6 – As opponent approaches, repel him with a kick.

    7 – Scamper on all fours to retrieve sword.

    8 – Opponent looms over you with sword raised high.

    9 – Grab sword in bushes just in time, grunt, and stab him or her through the chest.

SWORD FIGHTING ON A DANCE FLOOR

    1 – Draw swords.

    2 – Clash swords high.

    3 – Left foot goes back.

    4 – Clash swords low. Pivoting on right foot.

    5 – Lock arms with opponent.

6 – Swing your partner 'round and 'round.

7 – Do-si-do.

8 – Plant feet firmly and flip opponent over back.

9 – Opponent should land face up.

10 – Drive sword into opponent's chest.

11 – Clap hands.

SWORD-FIGHTING PRACTICE: ALONE

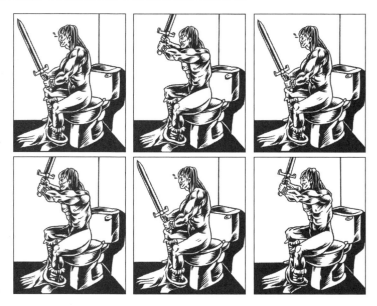

1 – Find mountaintop.

2 – Wave sword around in the sunset while flexing your biceps.

3 – Cue tracking shot away from you and across a dramatic mountain range.

4 – Or, see the diagram above.

SWORD-FIGHTING PRACTICE: WITH A FRIEND OR RELATIVE

1 – Repeat Steps 1 through 4 from SWORD FIGHTING.

2 – Do not repeat the other steps. Try to avoid killing your friend or relative.

BLUNT MELEE, ON HORSEBACK

1 – Ride through crowd of enemies.

2 – Bash enemies on head.

3 – Fall off horse.

4 – Grab sword from dead body. See SWORD FIGHTING (page 38).

AX

1 – Swing ax.

2 – Behead several enemies. Get overwhelmed.

3 – Stumble into a position where someone is about to kill you.

4 – Friend walks up and kills attacker with a dagger, OR, friendly animal walks up and kills attacker with brute force.

BOW-AND-ARROW

1 – Hide behind rock.

2 – Nock arrow on bowstring.

3 – Pull bowstring taut.

4 – Stand up to fire arrow at enemy.

5 – Let arrow loose.

6 – Repeat Steps 1 through 5 until you are out of arrows.

7 – Run at enemy and bash him with bow.

MARTIAL ARTS

1 – Face opponent.

2 – Disarm opponent.

3 – Punch opponent in face.

4 – As part of an unwritten agreement, your opponent dies, allowing you to move on to next opponent.

WHEN PART OF A HORDE

1 – Carry an ax, club, or sword.

2 – Ululate.

3 – Collectively charge at the enemy.

4 – Survive.

MUD WRESTLING

1 – Face opponent.

2 – Push opponent into mud.

3 – Slip and fall into mud.

4 – Wrestle.

5 – Try to get naked.

6 – This is the only type of combat where hair pulling is acceptable.

OTHER NOTES:

1 – Magic is for assholes.

2 – Armor is also for assholes.

3 – Wear sensible shoes.

KNOW YOUR VILLAINS!

The world has always been stacked against barbarians. Traditionally, barbarian[s] live nomadically, dwell among a small group of defenseless peasants, or trave[l] with feisty, bickering comrades. Their enemies, though, have mighty armies, hun[-]gry monsters, and probably black magic at their disposal. It's a tough world ou[t] there, and it's important to be able to recognize the defining characteristics o[f] your enemies so you'll know who needs to be slaughtered (your enemies) and wh[o] can be merely maimed (your friends).

EVIL WIZARD/SORCERESS

Public enemy number one is th[e] evil wizard. They're usually eas[y] to find, as they are fond of sinist[er] architecture and fire, and surroun[d] themselves with monsters and ter[-]rified, subservient peasants. The[y] also like to dress funny. The chie[f] danger is that they may use thei[r] magic to kill you. To complicat[e] things, these evil wizards/sorceresses are often your relatives, so if you ki[ll] them, you may have some explaining to do at your next family reunion. You'r[e] best advised to avoid them completely. Sure, it makes for a bad story, but it'[s] not *your* fault that the peasants got enslaved. Freedom ain't free!

Evil wizards usually have some sort of crest or insignia showing animal[s] locked in combat. This way, you don't have to be literate to find them.

BANDS OF FACELESS HENCHMEN

Bands of faceless henchmen ar[e] usually in the employ of a nearb[y] warlord, bandit king, or evil wiz[-]ard. Their goal is not to kill you, bu[t] to catch you and bring you to thei[r] leader so that he or she can kill yo[u] in some elaborate and pointles[s] manner, or sacrifice you to his o[r]

her false god. Your choices are to either slaughter the henchmen or submit to being captured, the latter of which can be handy if you've forgotten where your real enemy lives. If you don't want to be captured, don't worry: Faceless henchmen go down easily in simple combat. If they were any good at fighting, they wouldn't be faceless, which leads us to:

SELECT GLADIATORS, CHAMPIONS, AND OTHER BARBARIANS

These guys are skilled warriors working for your enemy and will put up a fight. Their objective is to kill you, usually in one-on-one, arena-style combat. If you don't think you can win the fight, you still have options. One option is to talk them into working with you by pointing out that their leader is evil. The second option is to lose the battle, but just as your enemy is about to step in and deliver the killing blow, let your friends sneak up and kill him or her. Option three is to save yourself with some magic device. But remember: If you use magic, you are an asshole.

ANGRY ANIMALS

Hostile animals usually approach in groups. Animals likely to attack include wolves, bears, rabid dogs, lizards, and anything you don't recognize. Nonthreatening animals include sheep, cattle, yaks, and horses. Some animals are in between—generally friendly but not to be trusted. These shifty beasts are called camels. Sometimes they are your faithful companions; other times they spit on you and the only appropriate response is to punch them in the face.

GIANT SPIDERS

A giant spider is very easy to recognize. Think of a normal-size spider. When a giant spider is very far away, it looks like a normal-size spider. Don't let your eyes fool you! As it gets closer, the giant spider will turn out to be much, much bigger. The spider's sole purpose is to eat you. You can defeat it by hacking off its legs, which will render it immobile and defenseless. As an alternative, crush it with a giant shoe.

MISCELLANEOUS MONSTERS

Monsters are, as a rule, extremely stupid. They are also extremely easy to identify since they don't look like animals or people. They don't attack in groups, they don't do anything clever, and they don't move fast, so the simplest solution is to stab them through the heart. Wear gloves, though—they may have acid for blood. Really, monsters are so ill prepared for fighting a barbarian that the battle is completely unfair. Afterward, you will be ashamed. Don't let it bring you down. It was all in self-defense, right? Or maybe *you* are the real monster! Food for thought.

SEXUAL PREDATORS

These bad guys are primarily a threat to female barbarians. Anything with two legs, flattish breasts and a penis is probably a sexual predator and should be killed on sight, or, if you're feeling generous, merely emasculated.

WITCHES

The female equivalent of sexual predators, witches will try to drug or magically charm you into submission. Don't trust any woman who offers you a mysterious smoky drink. This may lead to some short-term fun, but the long-term hazards include STDs, a loveless partnership, and ugly children. You'll also probably get torn apart and eaten.

ROBOTS

Once in a while you may encounter a gang of robots. Robots look like humans, but they are made of dull grey metal and have simple, clawlike gripping apparatuses instead of hands. They are strong, but slow and uncreative. The best way to destroy them is to douse them with water, but you can always just behead them with a sword or ax. The two great things about killing robots: 1) there's never any messy clean up, and 2) until the future, when robots will be self-aware, you don't have to grapple with complex ethical questions. Historical robots were steam powered, but modern robots run on electricity, which is a powerful form of magic.

Be wary of electrical shocks. A shock is that strange sensation where you feel very hot, lightning courses over your arms and legs, your hair shoots away from your head, your scalp gives off smoke, a warm yellow liquid runs down your leg, and you can see your own skeleton flashing white. Should you encounter electricity anywhere, run away at once!

BARBARIANS
OBSERVED

A MODERN STONE AGE FAMILY

Let's sneak a peak at a barbarian family going about its daily routine. It's a family of three: Boron Mouthbreather, his wife and sister Amygdala Toothpuller, and their young son Gûnto the Sheepskin Mishap. They are members of the Epokzi-Uptzi tribe, descendants of Reznälgh the Green, a Viking warrior who led a sea expedition in 1044 to prove that the world was sausage shaped. He managed to avoid seeing land until his oarsmen rowed all the way to California—no small feat. Upon landing, these nomadic Vikings pressed inland until they ran out of food and water in the middle of the desert, where they decided to settle. Flash forward nearly a thousand years, and they are now living right outside North Las Vegas, Nevada. They remain 99 percent Viking, mitochondrially speaking. Though descended from high-functioning barbarians, the Epokzi-Uptzi are considered a low-functioning barbarian society, probably due to their fanatical inbreeding. I observed them for a week, then left under cover of darkness.

Amygdala is typically the first to rise, at about six in the morning. She gets together with the girls and wanders off to a nearby lake to spend two or three

Gûnto the Sheepskin Mishap dreams of heavy metal greatness.

hours cavorting naked. She then dresses in her best torn leather bikini and spends the next two hours combing her hair, shaving her legs, and applying mascara, lipstick, rouge, blush, eyeliner, lip gloss, lip liner, and nail polish. For thousands of years, makeup and skimpy clothing has been the defining characteristic of barbarian ladies, and Amygdala could not imagine living any other way. The source of the makeup is a mystery guarded by generations of Epokzi-Uptzi. Boron believes it is made from crushed lizards.

Gûnto the Sheepskin Mishap, a boy of ten, spends his days avoiding his parents and playing air guitar with his friends. Gûnto actually owns an electric guitar, but it remains unused since the Epokzi-Uptzi don't understand electricity. Nevertheless, Gûnto is aware of heavy metal, and he dreams of being the lead singer of Dokken. (For more about barbarian youth, see "The Fate of Barbarian Children," page 54.)

Boron's day begins by executing a condor and smearing its viscera all over his pectorals as a symbol of glory. He then wanders off into the desert for a quick colon cleanse, wiping himself clean with bird feathers. On holidays, he will take a "whore's bath," rubbing himself down with guava juice. Unlike most desert barbarians, Boron's body hair is generously distributed across his barrel-chested frame, such that he can be mistaken, from a distance, for a giant hairball. Nevertheless, he insists on a clean-shaven face—surely his only act of male vanity.

Once they are all similarly toileted and groomed, the adult men of the tribe gather for their morning wrestle. They form a crude circle and take turns trying to mash each others' face into the desert sand. This tournament usually lasts about three hours. The winner is elected King for a Day and is entitled to stroke anyone's goat without fear of reprisal. The losers return to their yurts in shame and beat their children. Today, Boron is one of the losers. After roughing up Gûnto for a couple of hours, he feels like a big man, which, in fact, he is (I'm guessing six-four and five hundred pounds).

It's peacetime, but if the tribe were involved in a war, the King for a Day would direct his soldiers to vanquish their helpless enemies while Gûnto and the other children dug a vast pit for the corpses. The Epokzi-Uptzi are excellent swordspersons and archers, and have successfully protected their land for nearly nine hundred years. Although they don't have many adversaries today except strip-mall developers, they have historically faced other barbarian tribes, as well as cowboys, Indians, stagecoach-riding pioneers, and the mafia. As spoils of their

Amygdala's undirected frolic

previous victories, the Epokzi-Uptzi own the Tropicana and the Riviera casinos, although they have never visited them.

Sometimes, alongside the men's tournament, there is a mud-wrestling tournament for the women. Many Epokzi-Uptzi women have found work wrestling in Vegas in assorted viscous substances—whipped cream, margarine, macaroni and cheese, etc. Disappointing for me, as an observer, I did not witness one of those women's wrestling contests. Instead, Amygdala and the other women returned from their morning bath to make breakfast for the men. In a war, the women would be fighting alongside the men. Many barbarian women are skilled swordspersons, but a woman will not fight in a battle until she is properly dressed and has "put her face on." After preparing breakfast, Amygdala visits her mother, Porputa, who, like many elder barbarian women, excels at hexes, love potions, and three-card monte. They spend the afternoon yakking about handbags and shoes and different ways to murder Boron.

After food or battle, Amygdala retires to the nearest waterfall for a brief three-hour, undirected frolic. Since barbarian women spend so much time bathing, water pollution has torn serious rifts in their society. Some have taken to fruit juice or yogurt baths, while others have begun using hygienic products like soap and shampoo. Some even relocate to forests near trailer parks with shared showers. Water pollution is less of a problem for the men, who only bathe by accident, e.g., when crossing rivers, sneaking into moated castles, or falling out of trees into ponds while stalking women.

Following her afternoon shower and rinse, Amygdala joins the other adult women for their evening exercises: aerobics for cardiovascular energy, squats to tone their legs and thighs, and bench presses to enlarge their breasts. This is followed by a siesta at the nearest hot springs, relaxing their muscles and unclogging their sand-filled pores.

For dinner, Amygdala dines separately from the men on a light meal of horse brains and smoked goat jerky. As night falls, she wants to get as far away from Boron as possible. For his part, Boron eats everything within a six-mile radius, drinks a keg of beer or wine, and then usually tries to engage in rough sex with whatever he can get his hands on. Sometimes dinner ends with a midnight pillage of a 7-Eleven. Other times, dinner adjourns with games, such as sluggo, in which the barbarians punch one another in the face as hard as they can, or chess, where the players see who can fit the most chess pieces into his mouth. Boron is usually pretty tuckered out after that. With the cries of bleeding goats echoing through the village, it's time to sleep for about twelve hours before starting another magical day.

Once Boron has passed out, Amygdala streaks out the door, climbs out the window, or slithers up the chimney, if necessary, to escape to the Strip, flirting at discos and dives in search of men sporting bling. She is usually successful, but these are short-term relationships—city men don't want to bring barbarian women home to Mother. That's not a problem for Amygdala, who knocks the men out, if necessary, after her one-night stand, using whatever blunt instruments are handy on their nightstands—lamps, usually. Then she pilfers their wallets, cell phones, and, for some reason, their dish towels, and she kidnaps their pets to make light snacks for Gûnto. The proceeds from her thievery help pay for her classy makeup, stylish bikinis, and sensible but ladylike barbarian shoes.

As the rosy fingertips of dawn stretch across the horizon, Amygdala struts homeward in what is known among single barbarians as a walk of shame or, for married ones, a march of spite. Arriving at her squalid village, she leaps into a cistern and gets a couple of hours of sleep as her majestic, flowing hair spreads across the water's surface. And then the cycle begins anew.

THE FATE OF BARBARIAN CHILDREN

GRÜTE SAYS

If wife get pregnant, get new wife!

Useless in battle and too stupid for school, barbarian children exist only as a necessary evil for the perpetuation of the tribe. Historically, most adults would trade their kids to the Greeks for half a beer and then buy the guy who took the child off their hands another round.

Infant barbarians, colloquially known as babyrians, or the appallingly cutesy barbaby-rans, are particularly vulnerable. Savage societies have very little patience for long-term planning, and babies are demanding and not very useful. Their cries are signs of weakness, which parents view with the utmost contempt. There are many methods that barbarian tribes use to eradicate their kids, but they are too grisly to be described even in this book. (At your local public library you can find this information in *Infanticide for Dummies* in the Self-Help section. It should not be confused with *Dummies for Infanticide*, which is a small political organization in Texas.)

Barbarian children who aren't sold or snuffed spend their early years absorbing "lessons" (i.e., beatings) from their parents and training to make themselves productive warriors. If, however, a barbarian child's parents are killed at an early age by a rival tribe or an evil wizard, he may dedicate his life to vengeance for his parents' death, which is ironic, since most barbarian parents would murder their own kids if given an excuse.

A babyrian

THE SWINGIN'
SKULLBASHER WEDDING

On paper, Grüte Skullbasher comes across as something of a monster, capable only of bashing and bludgeoning. You would certainly take that view if you saw him repeatedly beat me over the head with a marble-topped credenza, something he's quite fond of doing.

It's easy to find examples of Grüte "acting out." Once, while I was in his care, he got a noise complaint from his neighbors. After he bribed the police, he busted into his neighbors' house and bit their parakeet's head off. He is fond of buying Italian Renaissance masterpieces and shredding them with a table saw. And then there was the time he burst into a cathedral during Mass, shouted "God is dead!," poured malt liquor on the transubstantiation wafers, ran up to the pulpit, farted thunderously into the microphone, and then leaped through a stained glass window and dashed down the street, cackling like a wicked witch. Another time, he pushed an ambulance off the George Washington Bridge and then torched the hospital it came from. Why does he do these things? I do not know. Perhaps I've been an anthropologist too long, or maybe it's my brain hemorrhage speaking, but I think these aspects of his personality can be overlooked due to an anthropological concept called cultural relativism. Simply put, it is the barbarian way, Grüte is an exemplary specimen, and who am I to comment?

But Grüte demands that I comment, and so I will. As his captive, I got to know him quite well. You wouldn't guess it, but he does have his occasional tender moments. Once, a little girl with a learning disability came to ask Grüte for help with some schoolwork. Her name was Carina Frumkin. Being illiterate himself, Grüte couldn't help her much with her book report, so instead he ran down to her school, grabbed Carina's teacher by the neck, twisted him into a pretzel knot, and threw every copy of the book *Beezus and Ramona* (1955) into a makeshift bonfire. Grüte then busted open all the lockers, liberating all the candy to share with the younger students and all the drugs for the older ones. He somehow got a Black Sabbath album to play over the PA system and danced a kazatski on a table in the cafeteria. By the time he was tranquilized by the National Guard, Grüte had become a local folk hero and Carina had gone from class laughingstock to the most popular eight-year-old girl in America. (Grüte is selling the movie rights to this story, entitled *My Barbarian*.)

Carina made a point of visiting Grüte while he was serving time in Attica and, on her first visit, she was driven and chaperoned by her conveniently single mom Verilia. The moment Verilia's breasts entered the visiting room, Grüte was in love. He smashed his way through the glass with his head, chewed off his manacles, and overpowered the prison security guards. Grüte, Verilia, and Carina then stole a Camaro and raced back to Passaic. It was a beautiful thing. They scheduled the wedding just two weeks later.

Barbarian weddings are not common. It's perfectly adequate for them to live in sin, tempting the licking fires of eternal damnation. Most barbarian relationships don't last long enough to get to marriage anyway, and there is a 99 percent divorce rate afterward. But Grüte is a king, and he likes to party. He booked a private jet and we flew to Vegas, then switched to camels and made our way into the scrubby desert, where there stood a few tents with the crimson banners of the Bunglorians flapping overhead.

It was an outdoor wedding. At two in the afternoon, when everyone started to arrive, the sun was high in the sky and it was 95 degrees. There wasn't enough bottled water, and everyone got instantly sunburned and dehydrated. There was no road leading to the spot they'd chosen, surrounded on all sides by high pastel cliffs, and no parking lot. Cars and camels were haphazardly left all over the place. Through this chaos, I noticed a pair of gilded elephants, which had dropped off some VIPs, being led into the cooking tent. To enter the ceremony one walked through the desiccated rib cage of a tyrannosaurus. On the tips of the ribs were candles that had been spilling wax onto the bones, but the desert wind had put out the flames. The skull itself had a taped sign: "Frumkins left, Skullbashers right." For seats, they'd yanked up some giant redwoods and carved pews out of them. When the sun crested the mountains, we'd be setting these endangered giants aflame for warmth. Grüte really thought of everything.

I somehow earned a seat of honor in the second row, groom's side, right behind Grüte's mummified father, Sporg Skullbasher, King of the Industrial Wastes. Next to his corpse sat seventeen women in matching gold spandex catsuits, who I thought might be bridesmaids, but who turned out to be Grüte's other wives. Behind me was row after row of Skullbashers and other Bunglorian royalty I met later at the reception. These were not your standard dime-a-dozen, convenience-store-holdup barbarians. There was Kerik Skullbasher Grüte's brother, who was born in a yurt and who rose up to become president of Moldova, and Rhonda Skullbasher, Grüte's aunt—now Lord Executioner for the state of Texas—who is not shy about brandishing her huge double-bladed battle-ax. Horvlad the Punishing Bear is another Bunglorian king, who rules a county in midwest Kansas, and he was there with nine wives of his own and their family dog, Jug, in a midget tuxedo. Hawk the Slayer was in attendance with his wife Hundra, seated near some assorted Cimmerians, Taarakians, Hyrkanians, and Mongols. Grüte's mother, Lasherpa, was serving ten consecutive life sentences in a maximum-security pokey, so her absence was honored by a sack of potatoes wearing a tiara and decorated with a smiley face drawn in crayon. (More on Mama Skullbasher later.)

Cromwang, the drink of choice for barbarians

The Bunglorians didn't wait for the party—they started chugging away as soon as they sat down with golden goblets of Cromwang, a blood-colored beverage that exceeds 200 proof, since it contains some sort of metabolized impurity-free super-alcohol. Some of their goblets were fizzing and corroding, causing Cromwang to shoot all over everyone's catskin tuxedos and bare chests.

On the other side of the aisle were the various Frumkins and their ilk. The disparity between them and their future in-laws couldn't have been greater. They seemed like perfectly nice people, albeit a little nervous. They were a healthy, good-looking, and successful lot, straight out of Central Casting for a wedding scene, so there is little to say.

At the start of the ceremony, Grüte stood onstage between two piles of skulls, his sword at his side, wearing a leather topcoat/loincloth combo and a helmet with gilded moose antlers. The priest was Tony Bennett, who is apparently licensed to conduct these ceremonies in Nevada, and who impressed me by never breaking a sweat. The best man was a hideous ape-man with a round golden breastplate. Opposite him stood little Carina, all smiles. Next to Tony Bennett was a golden amphora the size of an atomic bomb, filled to the brim with red wine. Verilia, wearing the traditional white wedding gown, marched to the stage with her father, Harvey, to AC/DC's "You Shook Me All Night Long," and the formalities began.

"Do you," Bennett crooned, "Verilia Frumkin, take Grüte Skullbasher to be your husband, overlord, and protector, without any binding prenuptial agreement, until such time as you get old and ugly and he casts you out, or you are overrun and slaughtered by ravaging hordes in the sandy savage wasteland of life?"

"I will fight at Grüte's side forever," she replied. "No gods will separate us. The rabid dogs of infernal oblivion will not tear us apart. Kill me and I shall rise from the dead to sustain our lifelong matrimonial conquest. I do."

"Do you, Grüte Skullbasher, take Verilia Frumkin to be your eighteenth wife, indulgent servant, kitchen drudge, mopper of bathrooms, scrubber of tile, fixer of sandwiches, and barbarian queen, until you get bored?"

The reply: "Let's do this!"

The ape-man passed Grüte some lead handcuffs and Grüte slid them over Verilia's wrists. She started to cry, they kissed for a second, and then he plunged his face into her cleavage and motorboated her boobs. The crowd stood up and applauded. Grüte hefted the gold amphora, Verilia tilted her head back, and he poured wine down her throat until she coughed and it spilled all over her face and dress. Then he heaved the amphora back and chugged a couple of gallons of his own. Tossing the amphora aside, he pointed out Verilia's spot next to the other wives, and she dutifully sat down.

The ape-man
presented the
handcuffs.

A magic
sword!

I don't remember seeing her again after that. Grüte grabbed me and the ape-man by the arm and hailed a few of his friends, and seven of us ran out into the desert to smoke some Stygian black lotus. We sat around a fire, roasting lizards on sticks. Soon my head felt like it had filled with helium, and I staggered away, out into the hot desert. Descending from the sky came a beautiful sorceress, shimmering in gold and naked but ensconced in the magnificent tresses of her own flaxen hair. She kissed me on the forehead and said to me, "Byron, take this magic sword and recover the Emerald of Xoxor from the Dark Wizard of Morgloth." Starstruck, I agreed to the quest, and I charged eastward, away from the sun, until I was set upon by giant green goblins who speared me with a thousand tiny swords. Then the Dark Wizard teleported before me. Still held by the goblins, I fought the wizard as valiantly as I could manage, stabbing at his heart, but my blows bounced off his chest. He started slapping me silly and suddenly my head cleared up. I was stuck to a cactus, and the wizard was Grüte. I had been screeching about the Emerald of Xoxor while trying to slice him with a rusty muffler. He was laughing his ass off and handed me another black lotus joint, and I was like, well, what the hell, why not. So I had another puff, and a griffin carried the two of us into the air and we flew over San Francisco dropping copies of Aldous Huxley's *Doors of Perception* (1954) outside the 1964 Republican National Convention, the one where they nominated Barry Goldwater.

I was pretty much back on Earth when we returned a couple of hours later. The party was in full swing, though most of the Frumkins had driven off in terror or died of heatstroke, leaving just a few of their younger men to hit on various leather bikini–wearing Skullbasher Amazonians. I witnessed two twenty-something Frumkin men conspire to make a move on two Bunglorian babes in matching tortoiseshell bikinis. The shorter Frumkin was clearly the brains of the operation, which isn't saying much. The taller Frumkin was so trashed his knees were weak, and he could only wobble, not walk. They made their way over somehow, and the short male pointed at his friend and said, "Hey, you gotta meet this guy. He's *the man*!" "Yeah," said the taller one. "That's me. The *man*!" The girls seemed unimpressed by this courtship display. They whispered to each other, then stretched their arms out to the Frumkin boys. You could tell by the Frumkins' wide-eyed responses that they thought they were about to get lucky. Instead, the girls caught them by the necks and bashed their foreheads together. Stunned, the Frumkins went down and the babes dragged them through the sand off into some hidden cave. It's always nice to see young women display such self-confidence!

As the party progressed, guests were treated to hula dancers, acrobats, and two mimes locked together in a real glass box. The elephants I'd seen earlier were now wrapped in aluminum foil, trunks and all, and were being slow roasted on telephone poles over a fire pit that must have been twenty feet deep.

↖ Grüte, Verilia, and the
Skullbasher extend family

There was no champagne, only Cromwang. One sip of Cromwang and you feel like your body has been placed in a vise turned by massive stone giants while you are being run over by a late-seventies station wagon. Your brain desperately claws at your eyeballs

GRÜTE SAYS

This was one of my funnest weddings. One wife nice, but many wife better! Know any ladies? Can always use extra wench!

for a quick escape route, and when you belch, green flames shoot out your mouth. Within seconds you turn into *that guy,* the one who yanks off table-cloths and trips over chairs while trying to fondle all the bridesmaids. Everyone at the party was *that guy* (except for Tony Bennett, who is Superman).

Around midnight Grüte's wives, those who hadn't passed out in the desert or run off for the night with other men, started fighting one another, and wound up falling into a patch of mud I hadn't even noticed before (this being the desert, I can only assume the mud was imported, or that that's where all the water for the guests went). Everyone stood around them clapping, swilling, and spilling Cromwang while the ladies pulled hair, clawed clothes, and smothered one another. Once they'd ripped their respective bodices off, the whole thing devolved into an orgy, which I won't describe at length except to say a good time was had by all.

That is, until we heard the sirens. Somewhere in the distance we'd all noticed a growing plume of dust, visible by moonlight and the distant glow of Vegas. The sirens became earsplitting as Grüte's mother, Lasherpa, arrived on horseback, closely tailed by an armada of black Crown Victorias. She'd busted out of prison to make it to the party. Lasherpa stands about six-five and doesn't look a day over thirty. She was wearing the remains of an orange prison jumpsuit that she'd shredded into a bikini. "Coward!" she yelled at her son. "Why you not spring me for party?" Grüte looked down at his feet for a second, but there was no time for penitence. He tossed her a sword. The Crown Vics skidded in the sand and suit-wearing federal agents popped out to take positions behind their car doors. The remaining Frumkins all headed for the hills screaming, but the Bunglorians stood their ground. There was still music looping over the sound system: Black Flag's "Damaged" on repeat.

"Surrender, or we'll fire," someone barked through a megaphone. Surrender is not the barbarian way. They reached for their swords and held them high.

"Go to fuck selves!" Lasherpa yelled back, and the feds started shooting.

Bullets were whizzing everywhere, plinking off desert stones and echoing off the cliffs. I ducked behind the pile of wedding gifts and watched the Bunglorians protect themselves. They'd swing their swords at each bullet headed their way and knock them out of the air. The din was horrendous. The Skullbashers and other Bunglorians charged forward screaming and overran the cars. They leaped on the car roofs, kicked the feds in the face, and knocked away the guns. The best ape-man jumped off a hood into the fray and ripped out a fed's jugular with his teeth, then beat another fed with the body of the first one. The barbarians were knocking the federales all over the place.

It was like watching the 1975 Philadelphia Flyers play a pee-wee team. Carnage and gore spilled across the hoods of the cars and sprayed into the sand. Everything was made even redder by the flashing squad car lights. When it was all over, the barbarians were fine, although a couple had some leaky bullet wounds. Lasherpa squeezed some of the corpses' blood into an upturned Viking helmet and offered me a sip: "Makes stronger!" She was so blood covered anyway, she looked like a demon straight out of hell. Then she planted her sword in the sand and shouted up at the sky, "Tonight we grind the bladders of tyranny for Crom!" and she slurped the rest of the helmet's contents. We cheered, piled the gifts into the squad cars, and ate the elephants. Then we jacked the cars and made a beeline for the Golden Nugget in Vegas to paint the town red with further festivities. I woke up a week later in Ciudad Juarez with scars on my pelvis in a bathtub full of ice.

Lasherpa is one tough lady!

FROM THE FRUMKIN SIDE, GRÜTE AND VERILIA RECEIVED

- a blender.
- a fondue set with expired Gruyère.
- a used Monopoly set, missing the top hat and all the railroad property cards.
- water-damaged copies of *The Lord of the Rings* movies on videotape.

FROM THE BUNGLORIAN GUESTS, GRÜTE AND VERILIA RECEIVED

- a now bullet-riddled chest made out of a dead panda, filled with ancient gold coins.
- the last Elven Mindstone.
- a sword that shoots lightning bolts, which would've been nice to have had during the fight.
- twenty tickets to Wrestlemania 27 in Atlanta.
- the Emerald of Xoxor (this really blew my mind).
- three voluntary sex slaves from Florida, although one suffocated in her wrapping paper, and another was collateral damage.
- the Amulet of Yendor.
- about $753,000 in cash.

BARBARIANS AND THEIR DOGS

Dogs may be man's best friend, but they are much more than that for barbarians. They are allies: fierce warriors in their own right, givers of warmth in the frozen tundra, understanding ears to talk to, and providers of delicious, life-sustaining milk. Here are some notable dogs and their barbarian masters.

GENGHIS KHAN AND KHAZAL THE BLOODBEAST

GUNAN, KING OF THE BARBARIANS, AND HIS DOG SPANKY

YOUNG GRÜTE
SKULLBASHER AND JOJO

LEONA HELMSLEY AND TROUBLE

BARBARIAN CULTURE

BARBARIAN MATHEMATICS

I would give you until the count of five if I could count to five!
—Groo the Wanderer (Sergio Aragonés and Mark Evanier)

THE BASICS

There are three numbers in barbarian mathematics: 0, 1, and 2. The rest fall under the concept "MANY!" which is akin to "all numbers from three to infinity." As you might imagine, this is not a very useful counting system, but it is effective in battle and in resolving rent disputes.

AXIOMS OF BARBARIAN ARITHMETIC

$$0 + 0 = 0 \ (\textit{The Obvious Axiom})$$

$$0 + 1 = 1 \ (\textit{The Other Obvious Axiom})$$

$$1 + 1 = 1 \ (\textit{The Confusing Axiom})$$

$$1 + 2 = MANY! \ (\textit{The Impatient Axiom})$$

$$MANY! + MANY! = \text{``CROM!''} \ (\textit{The Nonplussed Axiom})$$

ALGEBRA

Known to barbarians by its original Arabic name, *kareemabduljabra*, algebra has been a great source of frustration for barbarians since they tried to conquer Arabia but were confused on the battlefield by foes asking them to solve for *x, y,* and *z*. Barbarians therefore have a deep-seated hatred of algebra, preferring to solve complex problems by bisecting mathematicians.

If 1 + X = 2, solve for X   X = "Argh!"

TRIGONOMETRY

Barbarians also do not do trigonometry.

GEOMETRY

Barbarians are acquainted with wheels and, therefore, with circles and, even more indirectly, with pi. Unfortunately, they don't have decimals or fractions, and they can't really count past two. Consequently, in barbarian math, pi = MANY!

VENN DIAGRAMS

According to Grüte Skullbasher, this looks like your mom's butt.

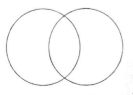

BARBARIANS AND PHILOSOPHY

What does not destroy me, makes me stronger.

—*Friedrich Nietzsche,* Twilight of the Idols, *1888*

Not a single barbarian has ever successfully read one page of Nietzsche. Based on my conversations with Grüte Skullbasher, though, I think they would definitely like his writings. This is the basis of my upcoming work, *Nietzsche for the Illiterate*, which will present Nietzsche's thoughts with the same instructional infographics you see on Heimlich-maneuver posters. As part of my research for this upcoming work, and in order to get at the heart of what one might call barbarian philosophy, I got Grüte drunk and stoned one night and bounced a few famous philosophical lines off him. It became clear that he is quite Nietzschean without knowing it. As a true barbarian, he remains obsessed with power, strength, and creating his own values, much like Nietzsche's Übermensch.

GRÜTE RESPONDS TO THE GREAT PHILOSOPHERS

PHILOSOPHER	SKULLBASHER
Religion is the opiate of the masses. (Marx)	Also football. People watch healthy athletes and get fat and stupid and eat nachos. They are weak fools—and fools die!
I think, therefore I am. (Descartes)	I kill, therefore my enemies are not!
Fear is the mother of morality. (Nietzsche)	Yes! Fear is a woman!
The unexamined life is not worth living. (Socrates)	Wrong! Life is for conquest, not self-exams!
And as ye would that men should do to you, do ye also to them likewise. (Jesus)	Men not have chance to do to me what I do to them!
Anatomy is destiny. (Freud)	Yes! Look at these muscles! My destiny is conquest!
No man is an island. (Donne)	Islands are stupid! Not many places on an island to conquer!
The great majority of men have no right to existence, but are a misfortune to higher men. (Nietzsche)	Yes! Little man get out of my way!
I saw under the sun, that the race is not to the swift, nor the battle to the strong, neither yet bread to the wise, nor yet riches to men of understanding, nor yet favour to men of skill; but fame and chance happeneth to them all. (Ecclesiastes)	Wrong, wrong, wrong, wrong, wrong, and wrong! Race, battle, bread, riches, bitches—all go to the mighty!
Barbarism is the natural state of mankind. Civilization is unnatural. It is a whim of circumstance. And barbarism must always ultimately triumph. (Robert E. Howard)	Yes! Triumph! Him smart!
A conqueror takes what he wants. The world fears his wrath and kneels before him like a whore! (Sung)	Mm! I tattoo quote on chest! Now go get me sandwich!

BARBARIAN CUISINE

Barbarians consume twenty thousand to thirty thousand calories a day. This may seem like a lot to you or me, but it's not so much if you spend your entire day running, screaming, and waving a club. Buffet-style restaurants are naturally popular. If you happen to be eating at a buffet and you see some barbarians walk in, you might as well call it a day. In ten minutes, there won't be anything left to eat. Also, they have no respect for the sneeze guard.

SOME BARBARIAN RECIPES

Move over, slow food. The newest fad sweeping the epicurean world is called "dis gustibus," and it's all about barbarian cuisine. There are five tenets of this gastronomic philosophy: catching your own food, never eating vegetables, crushing your enemies, serving only the nastiest bits of the animal, and smearing bone marrow all over your face and neck. If you're a kitchen klutz, or you don't have a high-pressure garden hose for rinsing mangled flesh off your walls, you can still find all these dishes served at General Ming's $3.99 Golden Palace Buffet in Manassas, Virginia. Be sure to leave room for dessert!

ROTISSERIE YAK (MONGOL)

INGREDIENTS:

1 yak, 1,600-2,400 lbs.
1 fire, many feet in diameter
1 tree trunk, big enough to support a 2,400 lb. yak

DIRECTIONS: *Build the fire. Uproot the tree and insert it into the yak. Spin the skewered yak over the fire for three days. Try not to stand downwind. Serves one.*

THE SOMMELIER'S TIP: This meal is best accompanied by fermented horse piss with a twist of lemon.

PICKLED HEADS (HUNNIC)

INGREDIENTS

The heads of 6 enemies

1 pickle

DIRECTIONS: Crush the pickle. In a very large bowl, mix the crushed pickle with the heads. Serve to your seventh enemy.

THE SOMMELIER'S TIP: After dinner, your pet ferrets might enjoy any leftover blood.

GRÜTE SAYS

Human head am have crunchy outside and gooey center—just like Tootsie Pop!

THE QUARTER-SUCKER'S FEAST (ATARIAN)

INGREDIENTS:

1 turkey drumstick on a plate

DIRECTIONS: Walk on top of the turkey to eat it. This is healthy stuff—it will keep your life force from running out,

especially when you need food . . . badly. Serves a Valkyrie, an elf, a warrior, or a wizard, but only one at a time.

THE SOMMELIER'S TIP: This goes great with a corked brown bottle labeled "XX."

GRÜTE SAYS

Remember, don't shoot food!

BROWNISH STEW-WATER (CIMMERIAN)

INGREDIENTS:

live dogs, hawks, snakes,
    camels, centipedes, etc.—
    whatever you can catch
enough water to submerge
    all the animals

desert sand, to taste
6 white truffles
some fire

DIRECTIONS: Mix together the animals and the fire. Let roast for six hours, then pull out whatever's left and drop it in the water. Let sit for five minutes, then strain the charred remains through a chain-mail bikini. (Pick out any feathers and fur and give them to your guests.) Sprinkle with sand and serve. Serves none.

THE SOMMELIER'S TIP: A large stone repeatedly applied to the forehead can offer the same delights as alcohol, but at a fraction of the cost.

SWEET DELICIOUS YUMMY PUDDING (MOK)

INGREDIENTS:

2 cups milk
1/2 cup sugar
dash of corn starch

1 equort heart
1 can Sterno

DIRECTIONS: Mix the sugar and corn starch in the milk. Remove the beating heart of your beloved equort (Discard the rest of the equort.) Place the heart in the milk solution and cook the mixture over the Sterno at a low heat until the heart stops beating. Serves one barbarian, one magical Chinese American princess, and one Mok.

THE SOMMELIER'S TIP: Only a coward drinks light beer.

LUMBERJACK'S DELIGHT (CALIFORNIAN)

INGREDIENTS:

1 lumberjack

ketchup, to taste

DIRECTIONS: Eat the ingredients.

THE SOMMELIER'S TIP: 375 ml of undiluted isopropyl alcohol, shot directly into your spinal cord immediately before starting the meal, might make this seem a little more appetizing.

TONY THULSA'S REPTILE FIESTA WITH LIQUID FUN SAUCE (STYGIAN)

INGREDIENTS:

3 cups chicken stock
2 tbsp. basil
paprika, to taste
650 ml formaldehyde
2 eyes of newt
1 throat of skink
2 anoles
1 Godzilla, boned

5 Komodo dragon
   thyroid glands
6 anacondas, 18 feet or
   longer, julienned
2 heads lettuce
butter—lots and lots
   of butter

DIRECTIONS: Boil the chicken stock, paprika, basil, and form-aldehyde in a lead pot (this will be your Liquid Fun Sauce). Meanwhile, sauté the newt eyes and Godzilla in a nonstick frying pan at a low heat. It takes nimble fingers to yank out the newt eyes, so if you're feeling lazy, go ahead and toss in the whole newt. The main course is ready when it turns a rich, pukish green and farts noxious gas. Mix the anoles, skink, glands, and lettuce in a large salad bowl. Dump the Liquid Fun Sauce over everything, and serve the meal garnished with the anaconda strips (coiled around the plates, if you really want to impress your guests). Serves eight hundred.

THE SOMMELIER'S TIP: Costco sells three-liter jeroboams of Pepto-Bismol.

BARBARIAN MUSIC

Whether beheading one's opponents with the flick of a scimitar, or lost in the frigid desert night with only a sneaky camel for company, barbarians have always loved their music. Coupled with montage, it's a cheap way of creating a sweeping dramatic feel without much dialogue or character development. Most barbarian music is orchestral, but there are a few spare fragments with lyrics that have survived from ancient history. Common themes throughout the barbarian musical tradition include battle, food, alcoholism, and love for one's animals or, on occasion, women.

GRÜTE'S THEME

Grüte Skullbasher used to sing this while cooking stew. The verse is repeated until dinner is ready to serve.

> Ya, ya, ya
> Gur, gur, gur
> Hn, hn, hnn
> boil a big fat raaaaat, yeah
> one more tasty raaaaat

GRÜTE SAYS

Grüte also sing when boiling cats!

OF ALL THE WAYS YOU SMELL

This is a Shemite love song from the Hyborian Age.

> Your feet smell like two oysters,
> left out for five hot days.
> Your hair smells like a stillborn goat;
> your breath like death's decay.
> Between your legs, the frontal side
> like dead fish on burnt toast.
> But darling, it's your backside
> that I love to smell the most.

CHRISTMAS IN BURKUBANE

Burkubane is the land of perpetual night. This song still gets some airplay in Burkubane's shopping malls beginning around Thankskilling Day and on throughout December. Burkubanians are rather emphatically non-Christian. (Lyrics by Gedren Hammacherschlemmer, 919 CE. Protected by BSCAP; reproduced here with permission.)

The skulls are all suspended,
and crowned with mistletoe.
And all the dogs
are disemboweled
and fed to hungry crows.

And all the angels torn apart—
their wings all plucked and boned.
And all the goblins
hum along
to Christian pris'ners groans.

All the minions of the night
unleash their banshee cries
to drown out the
Christian carolers
and all their sing-song lies.

Burkubane, O Burkubane,
your glow is none too bright.
Let's catch and kill a reindeer
on this unholy night.

Let's sacrifice to Thoth-Amon
on this unholy night.
We'll sacrifice old Santy Claus
on this unholy night.

MY YAK

This is the only surviving fragment of music from Genghis Khan's reign. It was rediscovered in 1958, during a State Department–sponsored visit to Mazar-i-Sharif, by Mel Tormé, who translated it from archaic Pashtun. Supposedly, Tormé's rendition was so good that it plunged Frank Sinatra into a year-long depression, during which he considered abandoning his singing career to become a rodeo clown.

He never worries if I come home late.
He never argues, he's very sedate.
He helps me plow the fields, and someday
he'll be on my plate.
That's why I'm crazy 'bout my yak.

GRÜTE SAY

Nothing come between a Mongol and his yak!

He never tells me to wash off that dirt.
He never says I need to buy a bigger yurt.
With other Mongols he never will flirt.
That's why I'm crazy 'bout my yak.

He loves that bright green, knocked-out, cuckoo,
groovy wind-swept grass on the ground.
He won't make a sound.
He's meat.
That's neat.

Won't tell me I'm lazy,
or make me rake leaves.
Won't say I'm crazy for what I believe.
Helps till the soil
unlike the rest of the beeves.
That is why I'm crazy 'bout my yak.

He's much more fun for me
than my seven wives.
He makes me want
to sharpen my knives.
Tell them get packin',
and run for their lives—
that is 'cause I'm crazy 'bout my yak.

Grüte Skullbasher is definitely the biggest fan of this appalling 1989 hard-core death metal single by the Soul Stomping Hell Red Toxic Demon Slaves of Murder Hell. In 1993, SSHRTDSMH went evangelical and re-formed (no pun intended) as a choral folk band, Christ and the Singing Redeemers. When he heard this news, Grüte was distraught and drank a fifth of Cromwang. Then he took a jet to Branson, Missouri, purchased a wrecking crane, demolished the Redeemers' recording studio, and pissed on the rubble.

You're tied in the dungeon of my dining room.
Nobody can see the crimson plumes
of splanchnic guts landing on my plate.
I munch your flesh and you taste like shit!

CHORUS:
Your leg . . . is going in my mouuuuth!
Your arm . . . is going in my mouuuuth!
Your spleen . . . is going in my mouuuuth!
Stop struggling, now I beat your faaaace!

Food for my belly is food for thought.
You are my food because you're what I caught.
You deserve nothing but this fork of lead.
A crown of thorns, shut up, shut up, shut up!

CHORUS (and screeching guitar solo):
The recipe's in the Necronomicon,
I kidnapped you at Comic-Con.
You were dressed as Princess Leia.
Roast in my stomach, you Star Wars slut!

GRÜTE SAYS

Song so beautiful it bring tears to my ears . . .

CHORUS:
Slay all the weaklings and the puny fools!
Burn all the florists and the Sunday schools!
Spray all the living with a hose of blood!
Spread my seed on your mother's face!

UNCERTAINTY

This is a rather recent entry to the barbarian-music canon, recorded in 2005 by the emo-barbi-core group Me Hurting Bad. Emo (as in "emotional") and barbi (as in "barbarian") were never a good mix, and the band's short-lived success ended in December of that year when all four members simultaneously decapitated each other in an orgy of self-disgust. In this song, the guitarist and bassist played one note repeatedly while the lead singer yelled out the lyrics and the drummer banged on the stage floor with a rock. All the songs by Me Hurting Bad were like that. *Rolling Stone* magazine described their one album, *This Loud Noise*, as "reminiscent of an atonal Cookie Monster singing alone while he waits for his running shoes to come out of the dryer," comparing the album to Lou Reed's *Metal Machine Music* and giving it five stars.

> *Me uncertainty*
> *about you feeling me.*
> *You feel my heart good.*
> *I also make feel your heart good.*
> *You make me want to eat big food.*
> *I hope you am not a dude.*
> *Me have got a real bad attitude.*
> *Cer-tain-ly.*
> *Cer-tain-ly.*
> *Me no have no certainty.*
> *I think I give to you the HPV*
> *because you give me leprosy.*
> *Stupid we.*
> *You and me am have hearts burn like fire on TV.*
> *You am want me state my goal;*
> *I want to piss in bathroom of your soul.*
> *Cer-tain-ly.*
> *Cer-tain-ly.*

GRÜTE SAYS

Emo??? Hear the lamentations of the wimpy!

TOQUAR THE INHALER'S GREATEST HITS!

Featuring all your favorites:

Ogre Face

Don't Stop Beheadin'

Fly Me to the Morgue

Blood Drops Keep Fallin'
   from Your Head

Nail a Mangled Liver to the
   Old Oak Tree

One Bourbon, One Scotch,
   and One Glogg

Addicted to Pus

If I Ever Loose My Blade on You

Single Ladies (Put a Rope Around 'Em)

When a Mok Loves an Equort

Like a Rolling Bone

A Yak with No Name

Act now and you'll also receive these patriotic ballads and ancient Brythunian hymns:

- Brythunia the Brutiful
- Gaguma Ta Lichbo Malkhezza Guz Notorgu Ghee
     (Bring Me Your Goats and Women)
- The Blood-Speckled Banner
- Crom Bless Brythunia
- Shehachhookh Galekchoo Gazuntheit-ka?
     (How 'bout a Quickie, Baby?)
- Gagumbo Gurganus Ocasek al-Cinder
     (I Stomp on the Toes of Your Pets)

with the talents of:

- Jeera abu Numkhazzedekh (high-pitched wailing)
- Melkhus Earpuller (whacking a calf-skin drum)
- Grungo, the Golden Stag of Perplexica
     (strumming a one-stringed instrument)
- Ambina, the Rust King's Sister (blowing a wind instrument)
- Shogthog the Unimpressionable (banging two rocks together)
- Turg the Syphilitic Coyote (howling)
- Some Horses (stomping feet)

All songs have been carefully demastered onto packing tape for a rich monaural sound!
A selection this good would regularly cost $1,599.95, but we're offering it for only $4.95*!

* *Offer not valid in stores, by mail order, or on the Internet. May be redeemed if you traverse the wild swamps of Kapongis (a mystical place with constant fog and undead mosquitoes), capture the Silven Unicorn of Bally-Hoha, slay Turjax the Beholder in the Keep of Vertiginous Misery, and bring the Goblet of Blaagit back to the mayor's office in Keokuk, Iowa.*

BARBARIAN LINGUISTICS: A LESSON IN MIDDLE STYGIAN

Many barbarians are still unfamiliar with English or other modern languages. Should you interact with such a specimen, in addition to their own language, they will probably know at least a little Middle Stygian (known to its native speakers as Barbarbushkaya). To get you started, the table on the facing page offers a helpful sample of a standard conversation in formal Middle Stygian, from which modern derivations can easily be conjugated. In this practice text, you are an organic grocer interacting with Slor the Hyena, a ninth-century conqueror who personally dismembered 157 Christian missionaries in Tunisia in 872 CE. For a more complete introduction to this ancient barbarian language, please see my book *More Than Just Grunts: Middle Stygian for Beginning and Intermediate Speakers.*

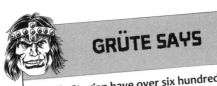

GRÜTE SAYS

Middle Stygian have over six hundred words for "disembowel"!

DON'T LET THIS HAPPEN TO YOU!

Dr. Byron Clavicle's *More Than Just Grunts: Middle Stygian for Beginning and Intermediate Speakers* is available from Insight Editions for only $139.95!

AT THE STORE: A PRACTICE CONVERSATION IN MIDDLE STYGIAN

SPOKEN MIDDLE STYGIAN	ENGLISH TRANSLATION
YOU: Naganga tawanga! Yorgh Thurman. Shalkhenky al «Thurman's Organic Superstore!»	Why, hello there! My name is Thurman. Welcome to Thurman's Organic Superstore!
SLOR THE HYENA: Arghhh! Thurman-gahh!! Yorgh Slor nal-Chhezkhallah!	Good morning! I am very pleased to make your acquaintance, Thurman. I am Slor the Hyena.
YOU: Umgah-fayezkh Barbarbushkaya argho!	It is always a pleasure to serve a customer who speaks Middle Stygian.
SLOR THE HYENA: Fluzgha maheck tish-tosh, blahazy furganga-keng!	Likewise, I appreciate your efforts to converse in my native tongue!
YOU: Snagh nyargh, yaaah-hechkhy pissto nal-tachbröt lovidovi-zag?	Can I interest your highness in our fine selection of fermented dog-urine aphrodisiacs?
SLOR THE HYENA (putting hand on hilt of sword): Agrahh? Nokhazy al-sheckhh-zag!?	My dear friend, do I seem like the sort of individual who would require an aphrodisiac?
YOU: Ha-yee! Malhaji bak nekhlekto, tahoush olfaxa gaz-schmelkzer.	Indeed! We receive many orders for them from gentlemen like yourself suffering from chronic body odor.
SLOR THE HYENA (drawing sword): Gaaahh!	Shall we continue this conversation over armed gladiatorial combat?
YOU: Klaatu zinjanthropi. Baltchain-askhagh golschmecky-shmeck-zag?	I seem to have left my broadsword in my other pants. Would you accept my wife as tribute?
SLOR THE HYENA: Naat! Malchenga parkishka tachbar rounbakh!	No! She belongs in the parking lot behind your store with all the other camels!
YOU: Malchhuzy, najuzzle Barbarbush-kaya. Fickity-fockity.	Gosh. I should have continued my Middle Stygian lessons. Inadvertently, I see I have made an error.
SLOR THE HYENA: Maglazha najuzzle malchaychay, Crom!	By Crom, it will be your last!
YOU (as you are beheaded): Aauugghhh!	Thank you for shopping at Thurman's!
SLOR THE HYENA (while beheading you): Hyarrrh!! Maghlaza berada tipto!	The pleasure is all mine!

BARBARIAN RELIGION

Most barbarians worship Crom. Crom, notably, is a hands-off deity, taking the idea of "helping those who help themselves" to its limit by never interfering in world affairs. To atheists, this makes him indistinguishable from the deities in other world religions, but a true Crom worshipper understands that, if anything, Crom actively works against those who pray to him the most. For one thing, such devotees are too busy praying to get anything accomplished, assuming Crom exists at all, which most barbarians doubt, despite occasionally calling out to him and making animal and human sacrifices in his name. Those who insist he is real readily concede that he would be annoyed if roused from his slumber by idiotic requests from the mundane realm of our Earth.

Another popular barbarian deity is Thoth-Amon, who is, overall, far more active in his attitude toward human life. His followers practice dark magic and make frequent sacrifices when there is an extra goat or two lying around. They are, notably, far more dependent on their god's charity than Crom worshippers. Magic, as Crom fans rightly point out, is lame and inherently evil.

A few barbarian tribes are nominally Christian, though their approaches to religion have always been somewhat antithetical to Church doctrine. For

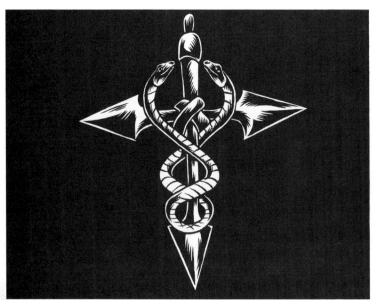

Thoth-Amon favors a standard with snakes (that are one) facing each other.

example, the Visigoths allied briefly with the Catholic Church, but rape and murder were prohibited only on Sundays, and Christmas was celebrated by gilding a heifer, placing it atop a mountain, praying at it for a few hours, and then going out on the town, to drub their neighbors.

There are various barbarian religions outside the global mainstream, but since barbarians are functionally illiterate, their holy books get more use as bow-and-arrow target practice and as umbrellas. Still, when there is an important decision to be made, barbarians will drag their holy book to the oldest woman in the village, who will furrow her brows in phony comprehension and then make something up off the top of her head.

The Holy Barbarella

A few barbarian societies do have rudimentary literacy among the clergy, most of whom attended seminary on track-and-field scholarships. Most of the holy books, though, are either bad translations of better-known books or sheer gibberish. Examples include the Moran and the Holy Barbarella.

Like its better-known cousin the Koran, the Moran forbids adultery and alcohol, but that's where the similarities end. The Moran forbids women from eating baklava, forces men to marry sheep, dictates the use of live scorpions as contraceptives, and requires 100 percent of all earnings to be mailed to someone named Captain Skunko in Khorasan. In 1103 CE, the Moranists realized that the whole book was an elaborate practical joke, but not before three centuries of holy warfare that claimed some thirteen million lives.

The Holy Barbarella, meanwhile, was an edition of the Old and New Testament that was translated *extremely* badly using the Codex Cumanicus, a sort of Italian-Kipchak dictionary, sometime in the twelfth century. It was delivered by the Byzantines to the Grundtli, a barbarian people near the Falah Sea in western Stanistan. The Grundtli were puzzled by mistranslated lines like "I, the Lord, am your rug burn," and decided some rewrites were in order to make it less sanctimonious and just generally punch it up for contemporary audiences. They may have gotten a little carried away. The resulting text describes acts of violence so depraved it actually makes the original Testament seem tame. What follow are some of the more popular excerpts.

Adam, Eve, and the serpent

GENESIS 3

Genesis 3:6 Following the advice of the serpent, Eve took some of the fruit and ate it, and gave some to Adam, who was with her, and he ate it. 3:7 Then the eyes of both of them were opened. 3:8 Eve screamed, "Holy hell, Adam! There's a god-damn anaconda in the middle of the garden!" 3:9 "Well, what do you want me to do about it?" quoth Adam, "I don't even have underpants, let alone gloves." 3:10 Said the serpent, "if I may ssssupply a sssssuggesssss-tion . . . ?" 3:11 Eve silenced him thus: "Shut your squawk-box before I taketh up a plowshare and slice you into snakeskin shirt-sleeves." 3:12 The serpent froze solid with fear, like an icicle. 3:13 The Lord came into the garden and snuck up behind Adam and Eve, and said, "Why didst thou eat from the tree of knowledge?" 3:14 Sayeth Eve as she spun around, "O, now *this* asshole again!?" 3:15 "What'd you just say?" spake the Lord. "Adam, this woman is but one of your ribs. I command you to keep her your captive!" 3:16 Adam backed off with a sheepish grimace and shook his head and made a slicing motion across his neck with his hand. 3:17 But Eve hefted the petrified serpent and held it with two hands before her breast and let out a fierce battle scream. 3:18 She charged at the Lord and whacked him over the head with the snake. 3:19 "This is going to end badly," said the Lord, running away backward. 3:20 "Yeah, for *you*," responded Eve as she gave chase and kicked at the Lord such that He lost his balance and fell prone upon the mud. 3:21 The Lord rolled over to see Eve raising the hardened serpent and ready to swing one last heavy blow upon his noggin. 3:22 But mercy staid her hand, and she merely kicked the Lord in the thigh. 3:23 The Lord scrambled to his feet. 3:24 Sayeth Eve, "Now get thee the hell out of my garden, and take your stupid snake with you, you patriarchal poltroon!" 3:25 She hurled the serpent in his face and saw that it hit his nose. 3:26 The Lord hastily vacated the garden, and the snake awoke and slithered away, and afterward neither didst trouble Eve anymore. 3:27 Adam also kept his distance.

DEUTERONOMY 20

Deuteronomy 20:13 [Spake Moses:] And when the Lord hath delivered this place into thine hands, thou shalt smite every male thereof with blunt truncheons. 20:14 Thou shalt kidnap the women and do unto them as thou wouldst not want done to thine daughters. 20:15 Thou shalt take away the toys and pets of the little ones and hold their wrists that thou make that they punch themselves, and ask them why they keep punching themselves. 20:16 Thou shalt burn down their houses and spew gooey spit on the smoldering ashes. 20:17 Thou shall eradicate everyone: the tillers of the soil, the butchers, the bakers, the builders, the labneh makers, the priests, the healers, the sick, the nurses, the midwives, the elderly, the writers, and anyone else I have forgotten in this list. 20:18 Then thou shalt rinse the streets with buckets of water and dance as shredded chunks of flesh drift into the sea as holy chunder for the whales. 20:19 Thou shalt eat the spoil of thine enemies, but only the unspoilt spoil. 20:20 After, we shall celebrate our victory every Wednesday. 20:21 But remember, bacon is out! 20:22 The Lord sayeth he would do all this eradicating himself, but he hath a headache.

KINGS 3

Kings 3:16 Two prostitutes came to King Solomon and stood before him, the first holding a baby. 3:17 One of them said, "I live with this bitch and she be sayin' this my baby. Now, I *know* it ain't *my* baby." 3:18 "Not *my* baby," said the other prostitute: "It *her* baby." 3:19 The baby was a naked boy and now he peed on the floor of the king's court. 3:20 "First of all," said Solomon, "can we get someone to mop that up?" 3:21 The first prostitute tried to hand the wet baby to the other prostitute. 3:22 The second prostitute threw up her arms and backed off: "Ah-ah, not my baby!" 3:23 The baby began to scream. 3:24 Then the king said, "Bring me a sword." 3:25 So they brought a sword for the king. 3:26 He then gave an order: "Cut the child in two and give half to one and half to the other." 3:27 "Works for me," said the first prostitute. 3:28 "Yeah, great idea, king," said the second prostitute, licking her lips.

REVELATION 13

Revelation 13:1 And a beast rose up out of the sea, having nine heads and fifty-seven horns, and upon each horn six crowns. 13:2 It looked like a legless camel with scales— let's call it a snake. 13:3 And it bled, but then it healed itself, and everyone thought that was creepy. 13:4 Men came to worship the beast, marveling at it and giving it power. 13:5 And one came to speak for the beast—an evil wizard. 13:6 And the wizard said all sorts of nasty, magical words. 13:7 And he waged war on the humble people who toiled in peasant villages as rakers of leaves. 13:8 And people came to worship the beast with him. 13:9 But there was one who was deaf, or maybe just reckless and stupid. 13:10 He grew up in captivity but somehow learned the riddle of steel and cameth upon a sword, with which he learned to kill. 13:11 Meanwhile, the beast and the wizard raised up some gladiators who were skilled and nameless. 13:12 These guys made sure that everyone said nice things about the beast and the wizard. 13:13 They burned more villages and piles of neatly raked leaves. 13:14 And they told people to make statues and trinkets shaped like snakes to look like the beast. 13:15 And they fashioned a standard with two snakes coming together, facing each other, and burned this symbol into people's hands. 13:16 There came a time,

The beast of Revelations and its wizard

then, when the deaf and/or reckless and stupid one was the only person without the mark. 13:17 And he fought for the rakers of leaves and slaughtered the beast and its followers until there was just him, his trusted sidekick, and the friendly ghost of his woman, which was already more people than he could count. 13:18 They celebrated by barbecuing some tasty vultures. 13:19 He was a magnificent warrior, and in time he became a king by his own hand. 13:20 And that warrior's name . . . was Jesus the Christ.

BARBARIAN
ACCOMPLISHMENTS

PORTRAITS OF GREAT BARBARIANS

GENGHIS KHAN (c. 1162–1227 CE) was the great leader of the Mongols, and without a doubt the baddest motherfucker who ever lived. Among his famous sayings: "The greatest pleasure is to vanquish your enemies and chase them before you, to rob them of their wealth and see those dear to them bathed in tears, to ride their horses and clasp to your bosom their wives and daughters." Damn right! Genghis is depicted here performing one of his less famous accomplishments: juggling three camels while balancing on a unicycle.

GUNDAR DUNDARSON, LORD OF THE GÜDENDÜDEN (824–868 CE) was a barbarian's barbarian who collaborated with Norse frost giants to wage war on Viking settlements throughout the mid-ninth century CE. Eventually, he was executed for trying to sleep with the frost giant king's daughter (seen here).

LUG THE OUTSTANDING (1361–1392 CE) was an overweight warrior who defended the people of northeast Khwarezm from the fourteenth-century Mongol conqueror Tamerlane. Standing six-eight and weighing over six hundred pounds, Lug used the power of never bathing to create a rich body odor so powerful that the Mongols diverted their armies hundreds of miles out of the way. Every August 12, modern Khwarezmians honor Lug's aromatic victory by burning car tires, brushing their teeth with anchovies, pouring raw sewage in the streets, and aggravating skunks.

FERGUS HEADBASKET (1961–) is the lead singer of the barbarian heavy metal band Pentacle of Pus. When Ozzy Osbourne famously bit off the head of a bat during a Black Sabbath concert in 1981, Headbasket viewed it as a personal challenge. In the middle of Pentacle's July 1981 show in Denver, Headbasket bit the head off a rabbit, which made headlines worldwide. Shortly afterward, Osbourne bit the head off an ostrich. But Headbasket was not to be outdone. In the middle of Pentacle's first world tour, Headbasket bit the head off their bassist. Osbourne quickly conceded defeat and retired altogether from biting things' heads off. Headbasket continued, however, and has now bitten the heads off an elephant, a blue whale, and all four of the stone presidents on Mount Rushmore.

GENGHIS KHAN

GUNDAR DUNDARSON

LUG THE OUTSTANDING

FERGUS HEADBASKET

CHOCOHOLOQETAL

CONAN THE ORANGUTAN

CHOCOHOLOQETAL THE SOARING TAPIR (975–2004 CE) was a jungle warrior from the ancient Yucatán who tumbled into an interdimensional portal and wound up in early-eighties Los Angeles. Speaking no English, he toiled as a dog walker until Roger Corman discovered him and paid him three dollars a week to work as a production assistant. His duties included raiding MGM to steal old Viking-movie props, crippling a gang of copyright attorneys, writing movie scripts, and torching Disneyland. He also played the slime monster in *The Warrior and the Sorceress* (1984). He died in 2004 of a cerebral hemorrhage while watching the Halle Berry *Catwoman* (2004).

CONAN THE ORANGUTAN (1906–1936) was immortalized in a lesser-known tale from Robert E. Howard's histories recounting the human Conan's camel caravan across the Hyrkanian steppe. Somewhere along the way, the barbarian let the orangutan come along, a decision he regretted throughout the journey. The simian Conan was a merry trickster, fond of running away with his master's sword. In the story's climax, the orangutan saved his defenseless master from certain demise by sneaking up and beheading an evil warrior.

TAARNA SPLEENMANGLER (1972–) is a Bunglorian actress working in adult films. She robbed a Burbank convenience store in September 2009 and then repelled a force of thirty-six LAPD officers using only a short sword. Her whereabouts are unknown.

TAARNA SPLEENMANGLER

THE LEGACY OF
BARBARIAN-AMERICANS

As the Marc Singer Distinguished Chairman of Barbarian-American Studies at Venice Beach University, I have enough facts in my head to write a whole series of encyclopedias on the topic of Barbarian-Americans—and that's exactly what I'm doing. So, in the interests of not repeating material I'm getting paid for elsewhere, here are some bits of research I couldn't fit into the *Encyclopedia Barbaricana*, which will be printed in 2013 in a limited edition bound in lacquered rat skin, and which no library should be without. As you shall see here, barbarians *are* America.

The history of barbarians in the United States dates back to well before colonists arrived from Europe. Native American tribes were for the most part highly civilized, but there were a few notable exceptions. The Cranquis, who dominated the Hudson River valley, for instance, were a real headache for their peaceful Iroquois neighbors. When Iroquois would canoe down the Hudson, the Cranquis would push boulders down from the cliffs above. They also liked to eat raw eagles. Hiawatha declared there could be no Iroquois confederacy without the extermination of the Cranquis. Though the Cranquis were not wiped out, they were eventually pushed downriver from the Iroquois nation to Staten Island.

When Columbus's epic voyage brought him to the New World, his boats were stuffed with able seamen: men who knew how to reef sails and sail reefs, how to prepare cat jerky, and where to find the tastiest ambergris. Real "arr-arr"–type barbarians of the sea, in other words. There were plenty of savage tribes to greet them on arrival, from the exuberant Discatecs to the cannibal Padawaks. Distinct barbarian groups don't usually get along, though, which is why the fighting began seconds after Columbus stepped off the boat in Hispaniola. In the colonial era, it's not clear who was more barbaric, the natives or the settlers, but as pig-eyed Columbus famously wrote in his diaries, "Civilization comes from the end of a gun." Since the New World natives had no guns, his victory was a foregone conclusion, and his seamen spread all over the continent, turning their attentions from spotting waves to whipping slaves.

After a few generations, the New World's barbarian origins were forgotten and the slow creep of antibarbarian bigotry began in full. The original draft of the Constitution stated that whoever a barbarian cast their ballot for actually *lost* a vote, on the grounds that barbarians couldn't possibly pick a stable candidate. Before ratification, the clause was removed from the Constitution to save space, because as James Madison famously stated in the Federalist 86, "barbarians don't vote. That's why they're barbarians." Some barbarians protested, causing quite a few cities to be razed, many colonists to be dismembered, and a few animals to be catapulted into brick walls.

The last major political protest by barbarians in America came in early 1841. William Henry Harrison had just become president on an antibarbarian platform. In response, the assorted barbarians in America joined forces and led a military incursion across the Potomac to Washington, DC, pillaging its restaurants, burning its libraries, and kidnapping its many prostitutes. Harrison was beheaded by an ax-wielding warrior in early April, shortly before the invaders were finally dispersed. It is one of the more striking examples of highly effective spin-doctoring early in Washington, DC's history that Harrison is remembered in history books as having died of a cold. (The whereabouts of his skull are still uncertain.) This battle is reenacted every Memorial Day, when bikers ride into Washington from across the country to pig out, ignore the bookstores, and stiff the prostitutes.

Antibarbarian bigotry continued throughout the nineteenth century. There was, however, a subtle countercurrent that began to form in the arts. Romantic writers came to view the solitary conquering hero as a mythic figure to be admired and emulated. For example, the powerful female leader of the Midwestern Zambonis is remembered in Henry Wadsworth Longfellow's "The Song of Biggihoho" (1855), a prelude to his better-known work about Hiawatha (see page 98).

Additional waves of European and Asian barbarians made the epic trek to America near the end of the 1800s. New York City was a popular place to settle, as it was the type of cosmopolitan city barbarians had always sought to destroy on their native turf. During this period, barbarians became the targets of much immigrant bashing. In 1898, for their protection and their exclusion, the U.S. government established several barbarian reservations throughout central New Jersey, Long Island, and southwestern Connecticut (it is no coincidence that World Wrestling Entertainment's headquarters is in Stamford!). The U.S. Supreme Court deemed these reservations constitutional in the trial *Brainmuncher v. United States* (1936).

THE SONG OF BIGGIHOHO

By the fi'ry Cuyahoga
Flowing into Big-Sea-Water
Stood the wigwam of Spumonis
Crusher of Bone, Spumonis.
Here the trees did laugh around him,
Here the trees with leaves upon them,
And the owls all started hooting,
At the sight of big Spumonis,
By the fi'ry Cuyahoga,
Pissing into Big-Sea-Water.

Then Spumonis stumbled homeward,
To his dark-eyed homely daughter,
Wayward bucktoothed Biggihoho,
Clad in thick flea-ridden leathers,
Ankles swollen like two turnips,
Face a mess of bites and pimples,
And they schemed to find a suitor,
Some young brave with lousy eyesight,
Who would never have to witness
Dark-eyed homely Biggihoho.

But in time she turned quite lovely,
And strong like teeth of beavers,
And she had her pick of suitors.
Hiawatha wasn't born yet,
So she settled for Lobacca,
Who ruled over South Dacotah,
Eating soy in South Dacotah,
Dull old boring South Dacotah.
Biggihoho told Lobacca,
"Let's move out of South Dacotah,
To a place with decent pizza."

So they gathered braves with arrows,
Who loved nothing more than killing,
And they swept through Minnesota,
And they swept across Wisconsin,
Biggihoho, dark-eyed sweeping,
Like a broom that gives out beatings,
For the honor of Spumonis,
Dear old dad Spumonis,
Fat old drunk Spumonis.

And at last they came to settle,
By the shores of Gitche Gotche,
Shining water near Toledo,
And they called themselves Zambonis,
And they slaughtered everybody,
'Til one day they got much older,
And they moved to Sarasota,
By the shining Big-Shrimp-Water,
Steamed spiced shrimp in Big-Shrimp-Water,
Shuffleboard by Big-Shrimp-Water.

Then departed Biggihoho,
Biggihoho the barbaric,
To the glory of the sunset,
To the regions of the nighttime,
Where the hurricanes are seldom,
Where the shrimp is everlasting,
At the all-night seafood bistro,
And the pizza sauce is perfect,
And they come with many toppings,
And deliveries are timely,
Everything is hunky-dory,
In the Land of the Hereafter!

In the late 1940s, Jack Kerouac took a road trip with Neal Cassady and a Barbarian-American named Zor the Implacable Badger. Kerouac wrote of it in his original manuscript for *On the Road* (1957), referring to Zor as "Hank Basho," but, due to antibarbarian bigotry, this material was cut by his editor. (See page 100 for an excerpt, courtesy of Zor's progeny.)

While racist and anti-Semitic laws were breaking down by the 1950s, barbarians were still almost universally despised and discriminated against. Senator Joseph McCarthy and the House Barbarian Activities Committee led an antibarbarian crusade, culminating in a series of trials that are, for modern mentalities, a little hard to stomach. For example, the trial of Asplundh Woodchipper:

JMcC: Do you now, or have you ever, knowingly lay waste to trading posts along the Silk Road in the Eurasian steppe, enslaving the women and ravaging the animals?

AW: Huh?

JMcC: I will repeat the question . . .

AW: Gyarrrr!!

JMcC: May I remind you, sir, that you are under oath.

AW: Nyarrghhh!

At this point in the trial, the defendant overturned his table, decapitated three lobbyists, maimed four senators, tore the clothes off a stenographer, and crippled a *Washington Post* reporter. He was ultimately deported to far Stygia.

Such discrimination continued in the United

Asplundh Woodchipper and Senator Joseph McCarthy

States until the early 1980s when Hollywood (and Italy) began making a conscious effort to raise awareness about the plight of barbarians. In the early 1980s, films like *Deathstalker* (1983) helped demystify barbarian culture and bridge the chasm dividing run-of-the-mill Americans from their oppressed

HANK BASHO PLAYED SAX

Dean and I and Hank Basho, this big tough bull from football, walked down to Birdland to see Will Gambino the great jazz sax man. Hank's shirtless all year round and wears leather and furs and boots like the queens of Chelsea but he only swings to jazz music. He carries a Louisville Slugger all the time. The bassist and the drummer played metronome sounds all quiet and then Gambino came out on stage slowly with his saxophone, long low tones, and the stage lights went blue like mad angelic heavens as the band jigsaw puzzle grooved, getting louder and faster, faster, all syncopated and I pictured a bottling plant and ordered Russian vodka for everyone. Dean started sweating, you could see it beading up around the collar of his red shirt and big red stains under his armpits spreading like beet juice. But Dean was quiet compared to Hank, the bennies were kicking in, and Hank's eyes were rolling back in his head and he started getting really worked up, beating on his highball with a fork, all rat tat tat, bim bam boom on the tabletop. He got louder than the band and someone put a hand on his shoulder and Hank turned and spilled his drink so Hank pushed the guy into another table sending wild sprays of redbluegreen cocktails catapulting through the yellow lights and sweatfog. Some people screamed. All the while Gambino kept blowing his sax and the bartender came out from behind the bar and started chasing Hank with this like mad flyswatter. Hank jumped up on stage and grabbed Gambino's saxophone and smashed the bartender over the head with it. The bartender hurtled back and the sax bell bent bad, then Hank put a hand on Gambino's chest and sent him flying into the drums. Next Hank started blowing on the sax. It was like the sound of a dying osprey, Hank couldn't play at all and the thing was busted anyway. I looked at Dean and Dean jumped on the table waving Hank's baseball bat and shouting "Go! Go!" Nobody even noticed, now there were drinks flying through the air and the band was hidden behind the bass. I walked up and yanked on Hank's sleeve and pointed at the door. We rushed through the bellowing crowd, out into the black-and-blue beatific Hell's Kitchen night, all whooping and cheering, and Hank kept blowing Gambino's stolen sax. Some police chased us and we ran like red imps. Hank took his bat and bashed in the driver window of a street-parked jalopy and Dean jumped in and fiddled under the steering wheel and the car fired up, booting out smoke and all bang bang under the hood. Hank smashed in all the other windows and we leapt inside and Dean jammed his foot on the floor and the car tore forward, we shivered from the wind and left the cops in the dust and Hank squawked on that saxophone all the way to Stroudsburg, then he chucked it out the window and it thundered on a road sign and all the suburban housewives put pies in the oven and turned on their televisions and trembled at the thought of men like Hank and me and Dean Moriarty as Hank slithered out onto the hood through the busted windshield and screamed up at the heavens, he screamed, "Don't you know that Crom is Pooh Bear?!" (*On the Road*, 1951 [published 1957])

savage neighbors. Still, playing a barbarian was considered a risky career move, and this attitude persisted until *Beastmaster 2: Through the Portal of Time* (1991) swept the Academy Awards in 1991, winning Best Picture, Best Director, all the technical awards, and the Best Actor award for Marc Singer. Thanks to ground-breaking movies of this sort, America is a little freer.

With many barbarians contributing to our present wartime economy as soldiers or defense contractors, the Barbarian Anti-Defamation and Swordsmanship Society (BADASS) has been able to put pressure on the U.S. government to recognize the rights of Barbarian-Americans. In 2009, the government issued an official press release apologizing to Barbarian-Americans for its shabby treatment of their ancestors. As a gesture of reconciliation, the federal government commissioned Frank Frazetta to create a statue of a barbarian, with his sword aloft, buxom wife clinging to his side, atop a pile of dead Taliban insurgents. Frazetta died in 2010 before completing this masterwork, so it was completed by Boris Vallejo and erected on American soil as far away from Washington as possible, in downtown Talofofo, Guam.

Thus, while the barbarian origins of our country are mostly forgotten, efforts like Hollywood's barbarian-movie renaissance, BADASS's current lobby, and my own scholarship are gradually influencing the public's awareness and political discourse. As President Barack Obama sagely observed at the Frazetta-Vallejo statue's dedication (via teleconference), "We are all barbarians now. *Hyyyaaaaggh!*"

BARBARIAN-AMERICAN POLITICIANS

Several U.S. presidents and government leaders have been of demonstrably barbarian origins:

- President George Washington (Scythian)
- President Franklin "the Eye of the Hawk" Pierce (Stygian)
- President Ulysses "Skeletor" Grant (Eternian)
- President Rutherford "Barbarian" Hayes (Cimmerian)
- Supreme Court Justice Thurgood "Dragonslayer" Marshall (Atarian)
- Senator "Savage" Estes Kefauver (Mok)
- House Speaker "Eye of" Newt Gingrich (Republican)
- President George W. Bush, on his mother's side (Bunglorian)

BARBARIAN SCIENCE AND ENGINEERING

When surveying ancient barbarian civilizations, one question is unavoidable: How were such amazing cities constructed by people who couldn't find their own asses with a map? Furthermore, complex construction requires management. Laborers or slaves didn't just transport huge stones across great distances and lift them for the hell of it—they worked under the orders of oppressive foremen or slave masters. Such hierarchy is antithetical to the nomadic ways of barbarianism.

It was only recently that scientists at the University of Chicago unlocked the secret of barbarian construction. "The answer," according to Dr. Hubert Dingle-burger, "is in the stones themselves." Barbarian stones were not found and transported—they were manufactured! In their stone-making process, barbarians soak strips of wet parchment in a flour-and-water solution and layer the strips over some sort of frame (or even rubber balloons). These husks are dusted with sand to give them a rugged stone-like color and texture and left to dry and harden overnight. After twenty-four hours, the barbarians have lightweight stones suitable for building cities! As a bonus, the falling rocks from collapsing walls don't actually hurt anyone.

Barbarian stones

OTHER GREAT BARBARIAN INVENTIONS

TANNING OIL

This potent poultice was invented by the Cimmerians in 6300 BCE. Ever since then, they've looked terrific all year round. The long-haired Cimmerians also invented conditioner, which they made by mixing curdled zebu milk and phlegm.

THE SCHWINGLESS SCABBARD

Generally, a sword pulled from its scabbard makes a *schwing* sound. When barbarians draw their swords, however, no sound is made (my point of reference here are the scores of barbarian movies where swords are drawn in utter silence). Although truly remarkable, the schwingless scabbard seems to be a simple fact of barbarian life, as no one ever calls attention to it. Scientists have

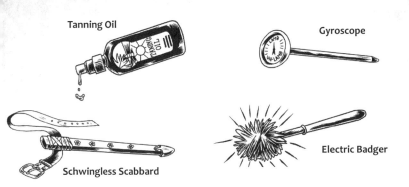

Tanning Oil

Gyroscope

Schwingless Scabbard

Electric Badger

also deduced that barbarians must have a steel-like cardboard material, evident from the *clank* that cardboard swords make when striking each other in barbarian movies. But the existence of such a substance is much more difficult to confirm than the schwingless scabbard.

THE ELECTRIC BADGER

This device is neither electric, nor does it resemble or function like a badger in any way. It is actually a brush for cleaning latrines. It is impossible to verify if barbarians actually invented this device, but they like to claim that they did. Putting the word "electric" in front of anything makes it sound cool to barbarians. They were big fans of the television series *The Electric Company* (1971) and *Breakin' 2: Electric Boogaloo* (1984), despite the critical panning of the latter. Grüte still listens to the soundtrack on occasion.

THE GYROSCOPE

No, not the device for maintaining stability. The barbarian gyroscope is a handheld tool used for measuring the percentage of lamb content in the slow roasts proffered by sidewalk mystery-meat vendors.

HANG GLIDERS

As with Leibniz's and Newton's simultaneous invention of calculus, nobody is sure which barbarian first invented hang gliders. Historians unanimously agree, though, that it was either Ator,

Hang Glider

the Fighting Eagle, or Yor, the Hunter from the Future.

BARBARIANS
AND
MODERN LIFE

CAREER OPPORTUNITIES FOR BARBARIANS

Over the past few millennia, barbarian career opportunities have subtly shifted with modernity to reflect society's new focus on information. It becomes harder and harder for muscle-bound, illiterate hulks to find a job. By contrast, thanks to a universal tradition of sexism, jobs for savage women have remained every bit as dignified as slavery has ever been.

JOBS FOR BARBARIAN MEN AND WOMEN

MEN

IN YE OLDEN TYMES
- Animal wrangler
- Blacksmith
- Conqueror
- Destroyer
- Raker of leaves
- Tiller of soil
- Warrior

IN YE MODERNE TYMES
- Bodyguard
- Football player
- Lumberjack
- Nightclub bouncer/bodyguard
- Politician
- Product stress-tester
- Stuntman
- Wrestler (or American Gladiator)
- Politician

WOMEN

IN YE OLDEN TYMES
- Bar wench
- Milkmaid
- Priestess
- Seamstress
- Servant
- Slave wench
- Slut

IN YE MODERNE TYMES
- Candygram messenger
- Dental hygienist
- Jell-O wrestler
- Naughty maid
- Naughty nurse
- Softball player
- Stewardess
- Tax auditor
- Wench

Raking leaves

Stress-testing products

BARBARIANS AND THE CITY

The following e-mail chain was forwarded to my assistant by a friend of a late-twentysomething woman who works in acquisitions for a major U.S. publishing house. The names have been changed.

From: "Tammy Cugartini" <t.cugartini@definitehouse.com>
Date: October 17, 2010 09:31:39
To: "Wanda Wuchinsky" <wawawuwu@hotmalez.com>
Subject: the divine sex secrets of the jaguar

Dearest Wanda,
Greetings from New York. I hope all is well. I'm writing you with some news that would have seemed tragic and ice cream worthy a year ago but was really a blessing in disguise. I broke up with Kippie! OK, don't panic yet. It's not as big a deal as it sounds. One night we were in bed and we had just finished our five-minute "love-making session" and I fell asleep, unsatisfied as usual (since it's over, I might as well tell you that Kippie had the sex skills of a fifteen-year-old). I woke up an hour later expecting to be in Kippie's arms and found he wasn't in bed. I went into the other room and he was there in front of the TV, playing with his Wii! I was horrified. Long story short, I kicked him out and called a locksmith to change the locks. By the time that was done, it was 2 a.m. By now I was wide awake and instead of plowing through a box of Mallomars and watching C-SPAN's *Book World*, I just decided to throw on some spandex and blow off steam at my all-night gym.

OK, I know you're like me, and after a big breakup you're not thinking, "Another year and a half down the drain . . . now I have to start over in search of someone to raise a family with." The big concern is, "What if I never have sex again?" So you're filled with doubts and the brain is running on overdrive with what-ifs. And being in a gym filled with sweaty pheromones makes things maybe a little worse. I mean, let's

GRÜTE SAYS

She sound like psycho camel in heat! Unsubscribe!

face it, everyone there is there to become more attractive, but the people you see there at that kind of hour are all weirdo night owls or actors or unemployed—so they're not exactly top of the breeding chain.

But then I spotted this one guy on the treadmill. I don't know how I missed him because he was totally shirtless and wearing these ragged leather shorts (or sort of a kilt . . . well, a skirt really) and fur leggings. He was golden like a roast turkey, and had long blond hair with highlights like a grunge rocker and a couple braids, but he was wearing this brass headband and had a totally clean-shaven body. And OMG he was huge! He was as broad as the treadmill was long. His butt cheeks were like overinflated basketballs, strong and solid. His legs were as big as my whole body. I drifted by and saw on the display that he'd run eight hundred miles—and he was barely even sweating! He looked less like a human being and more like a parody sculpture of what a human being would look like if he ate anabolic steroids for breakfast, lunch, dinner, and midnight snacks.

I finally saw him turn off the machine and wipe himself down with a towel, so I timed my exit so we'd get into the elevator together. But once he got in, there was barely room for me. I managed to squeeze in, though, and asked him to press 1. He could hardly see me over his own pectorals. They must have been at least a 48-D. I asked him his name. He said it was Murdok, the Sword of the Jaguar. I told him I'm Tammy and asked for his number and if he'd want to get a bite to eat sometime (I wanted to get him home right then but I'm not a *total* slut!).

"Me," he grunted, and banged his fist on his chest. "No have phone."

"E-mail?"

He shook his head.

"So how do people get in touch with you?"

He turned toward me, or where he thought I was, and said, "If they look for me, I find *them*." (I kind of liked that response.) "Where you live?" he asked.

"I live in the Phoenix on Greenwich and Bleeker. Apartment 17-A." I couldn't help myself!

"How it spell?"

I scribbled it as best I could on a piece of paper. My hands were shaking and there wasn't room to move my arms. He looked at the paper and held it upside down. I noticed just then that he was also a little cross-eyed, but who cares?

We got out of the elevator where there's the reception booth and there are full-wall mirrors on both sides leading to the doors. I saw him check me out in the mirror and smile. (I also saw the reception guy, no ninety-eight-pound weakling himself, leap behind the desk to cower.) When we got outside, I said good night to Murdok, the Sword of the Jaguar, and he patted his chest and put his leg up on a fire hydrant and squinted up at the full moon. It was cold out and he was still shirtless. You could have cut glass with his nipples. I backed off and started heading home to see my other boyfriend, Mr. Jackhammer 40,000. When I turned to look back, Murdok, the Sword of the Jaguar, was still staring at the moon. Well, OK, whatev—evidently he's not a werewolf.

So the next day, when I got home from work, he was there squatting in the lobby with the same leather skirt-thing and furry boots and he had his broadsword jammed into the carpet. The doorman said he couldn't get Murdok, the Sword of the Jaguar, to leave. It was Friday and you know I usually dress a little less professionally (or *more* professionally, ha-ha) on Fridays so I was wearing this kind of low-cut shirt and a silvery push-up bra and the shirt kept slipping down and showing the edges of the bra. Murdok took one look at my boobs and threw me over his shoulder and took me up the staircase, ignoring the doorman, who kept insisting that All Visitors Must Sign In. Seventeen flights of stairs will keep you fit, that's for sure. He only banged my head on the wall a couple times. I didn't mind. Then we got to my apt and he kicked in the door before I finished fishing through my purse for the keys.

I offered him a drink, but he just hurled me onto the bed and ripped off my clothes. He didn't even need to take off his own clothes (it turns out that he does not like to be, shall we say, constrained). I won't go into the gooier details, but I came like a volcano. When it was all over, the bed was nothing but a smoldering crater. Murdok, the Sword of the Jaguar, slept for fourteen hours, then woke up and we did it again six times before late breakfast and another six times before lunch (which was at midnight)! Never had so many 'gasms in my life! I think I'm in love. Also, I came three times while writing this e-mail. OMG, I feel like such a slut and I'm lovin' it.

BTW, when the NYPD finally showed up that night (because of the doorman), I told them it was OK. They asked about a disturbance and the busted door but Murdok, the SOTJ, stepped out and stamped his foot and they scattered. :P

Urs 4-ever,
Tammy

From: "Wanda Wuchinsky" <wawawuwu@hotmalez.com>
Date: October 20, 2010 18:27:12
To: "Tammy Cugartini" <t.cugartini@definitehouse.com>
Subject: Re: the divine sex secrets of the jaguar

Dear Tambo, skimmed ur long e-mail, sounds like a good rebound at least.
Don't get urself hurt, guys like that can be hard to get rid of. Sorey 4 the
shortie, but no news here, xoxoxoxo.
    -yer LA woman Wanda

From: "Tammy Cugartini" <t.cugartini@definitehouse.com>
Date: October 25, 2010 11:54:22
To: "Wanda Wuchinsky" <wawawuwu@hotmalez.com>
Subject: Re: Re: the divine sex secrets of the jaguar

Dear Wanda,

Haven't been to the gym in days but have never been fitter. :)
Get rid of him? OMG, no freakin way! Today I found out that Murdok, the
Sword of the Jaguar, has about a dozen other girlfriends. That's normal in New
York since we just started dating, but I don't think it is going to change even in
a year or two. But I'm gonna let you in on a little secret and I want you to tell
me I'm not crazy. ** I'm okay with it .** There's more than enough of him to
go around and I just can't imagine going back to dating dingle-dicks like Kippie
after this, even if they do make six-figure salaries and take me to Babbo every
night. MTSOTJ keeps calling me Taramis and that doesn't bother me, either. I
kind of like it, even if it sounds like a Greek salad. I'm moving in with him and
seven of the other girls. We sleep in a giant bed of hay wrapped in the fur of a
hundred alpacas (surprisingly firm + comfortable), down by 2nd and 2nd ave in
the Lower East Side (MTSOTJ loves borscht and vareniky). Found out he gives
private fencing lessons in Central Park. It probably doesn't pay well, but that's
OK. He doesn't pay rent, he just throws the landlord down the stairs.

    Xoxo 4ever, Tambo

From: "Wanda Wuchinsky" <wawawuwu@hotmalez.com>
Date: October 30, 2010 19:46:26
To: "Tammy Cugartini" <t.cugartini@definitehouse.com>
Subject: Re: Re: Re: the divine sex secrets of the jaguar

Dear Tammy, whatever floats ur boat babe. I got laid off yesterday. So sick of
all these nitwits in LA, coming back to NYC, hope there's room for another at
your place. Sorry 4 the brief note as usual, xoxoxoxo. —W

From: "Tammy Cugartini" <t.cugartini@definitehouse.com>
Date: November 10, 2010 8:51:11
To: "Wanda Wuchinsky" <wawawuwu@hotmalez.com>
Subject: Re: Re: Re: Re: the divine sex secrets of the jaguar

Dear Wanda, haven't checked phone or e-mail for days or gone to work,
but yes, totes, there's plenty room for more. Forget legalizing gay marriage—
I want them to legalize polygamy! Hey, it's OK in the Torah right???
    Murdok the Sword of the Jaguar sez he "be look forward of meet you." :)
    Love ya,
    Taramis, the Sheath of the Jaguar

GETTING INTO THE
BARBARIAN LIFESTYLE

ust as many of us like to dabble in black magic or light bondage, many people seek opportunities to explore barbarianism without committing to the solitary, poor, nasty, brutal, and short life that comes with it. Here are some ways you can meet some real barbarians and even try out some barbarian activities, without committing to all the discomforts of the true lifestyle.

PLACES TO MEET REAL BARBARIANS

- In a police holding cell
- Hanging out with Roger Corman
- At the gym
- Raiding a Renaissance faire (But watch out for LARPers—live-action role players—who are only pretending to be barbarians.)

- Wherever MTV is doing a casting call for a new reality show
- The Craigslist "Brutal Encounters" section
- In the parking lots outside heavy metal band reunion concerts
- Australia

WAYS TO EXPLORE YOUR BARBARIAN SIDE

- Get together with a few friends, grab some two-by-fours, and launch a raid on the adjacent town, hacking to pieces anyone who stands in your path. Steal their livestock and jewelry, and then bulldoze the whole place.
- Visit scenic New Jersey!
- Punch a camel or some other defenseless animal.

- Wait outside a religious ceremony and then crucify the attendees.
- Play D&D. (But remember: Clerics and mages are pussies.)
- Burn down the library or bookstore where you got this book. That'll show 'em!

THE BAT
(BARBARIAN APTITUDE TEST)

This test is designed to assess an individual's potential to renounce civilization and embrace barbarianism. You have sixteen hours to complete the following twenty-four questions.

ANALYTICAL
Think about the question, then choose the most barbaric answer.

1. You are sleeping behind a rock on the steppes of Cimmeria when you are awakened by the thundering hoofbeats of an Asiatic cavalry horde. You should
- **(A)** crush your enemies.
- **(B)** see them driven before you.
- **(C)** hear the lamentation of the women.
- **(D)** do all of the above.

2. You arrive at your office building, only to discover that someone has left his Volkswagen Beetle in the parking spot reserved for your Arabian stallion. You should
- **(A)** wait for the owner and attempt to reason with him.
- **(B)** urinate on the car and then run away.
- **(C)** yell "It's a machine!" and try to gouge out the headlights.
- **(D)** behead the owner, kidnap the receptionists, burn the building to the ground, and eat the car.

3. An evil wizard has captured a princess. In his castle there is an octagonal room with a mirror on each wall, numbered one through eight. The wizard is hiding behind one of the mirrors, and there are giant apes behind five of them. You swing at the second mirror and the seventh mirror and strike only one ape. One of the apes smashes through its mirror and rushes out to join another ape. A third ape is poised behind the fifth mirror, which is directly across from the second mirror. Which mirror is the wizard behind?

(A) Huh?

(B) I, um . . . Ugh. Mirror two?

(C) I smash all the mirrors, bludgeon the wizard, dismember the apes, and "marry" the princess before returning her to her parents.

(D) This answer sounds plausible enough. I will select it by process of elimination.

4. An evil bandit has taken over your girlfriend's castle. Unfortunately, inside the castle there is a weapon capable of destroying the world, and the bandit seems intent upon using it. You must stop him. The castle is guarded on all sides, but it has a secret entrance. What's the best way to get inside?

(A) Disguise yourself as a beggar and hobble through the front gate undetected.

(B) Send one of your more expendable friends to the front door while you enter through the secret entrance, dressed as a janitor.

(C) Wander off into the bushes and build a hang glider, and soar over the parapets, dropping Molotov cocktails on the guards.

(D) Don't bother, knowing that the bandit won't destroy the world, since that will leave him with no place to live.

5. An army of enemies has surrounded you, and all you have is your sword. You should

(A) panic.

(B) surrender.

(C) keep calm and carry on fighting, knowing they will always attack you one at a time.

(D) kill yourself and hope your friends know how to bring you back to life.

VERBAL I: ANALOGIES

This section apparently analyzes your ability to understand metaphor and similes.

6. pusillanimous : slaughtered :: pulchritude : _____
- **(A)** aghhh
- **(B)** grmmm
- **(C)** Nyaaaagh!
- **(D)** inseminated

7. frappuccino : feminine :: iPad : _____
- **(A)** virile
- **(B)** girly
- **(C)** Shut up!
- **(D)** Smash!

8. goat : stroke :: enemy : _____
- **(A)** dismember
- **(B)** kill
- **(C)** eat
- **(D)** Any of the above.

9. rubber : sex :: _____
- **(A)** sheath : sword
- **(B)** syphilis : avoided
- **(C)** oil : body
- **(D)** Yaaauggh! : Crom! What is this "rubber" of which you speak?

10. Sword : Sorcerer :: _____
- **(A)** Conan : the Barbarian
- **(B)** Warrior : Sorceress
- **(C)** Mark Wahlberg : Funky Bunch
- **(D)** inveigle : civilization

11. fur : Ookla :: Princess Ariel : _____

   (A) Thundarr

   (B) melons

   (C) spandex

   (D) delicious caramel skin tones

VERBAL II: FILL IN THE BLANK(S)

Even though you may talk like the following questions read, words have been left out of them. Try to put the right words back in to make complete sentences.

12. We thundered across the plains, _____ the villages
   and _____ the animals.

   (A) erecting . . . stroking

   (B) avoiding . . . raping

   (C) pillaging . . . slaughtering

   (D) burning . . . burning

   (E) enslaving . . . catapulting

13. Our people were devastated by _____. We have come for
   your _____ and _____ .

   (A) the Black Plague . . . milkshakes . . . dollar menu

   (B) rent . . . singers . . . dancers

   (C) cookie monsters . . . peanut butter . . . jelly

   (D) STDs . . . penicillin . . . Valtrex

   (E) your brochure . . . overweight women . . . discount
   electronics

14. The wrath of our local bloodthirsty warlords has been set upon us!
   Everybody _____ !

   (A) sacrifice animals

   (B) sacrifice other people

   (C) rake leaves

   (D) prepare for battle

15. _____ as she tore off her steel brassiere to release those captivatingly large breasts.

(A) "Hey, get a load o' these!" Kee-Ra exclaimed,

(B) Gondar could only think of his dead mother

(C) "A Hollywood producer, right here in Samarkand! What luck!" she squealed,

(D) "I know I left my car keys down in here somewhere," she muttered,

(E) "Two snakes coming together, facing each other, like this," she grunted,

16. We found the book about barbarians to be _____ and _____ .

(A) delicious . . . nutritious

(B) informative . . . tasteful

(C) puerile . . . Pulitzer worthy

(D) ingenious . . . flammable

(E) better than Alvin . . . the Chipmunks

VERBAL III: READING COMPREHENSION

The questions below pertain to the following passage. Read the passage and answer the questions. Or, cheat off the sheet of whoever is sitting next to you.

As she gazed upon the Fortress of Loxar high on the hill, Amagina knew it was a trap. She could sense the slithering hobgoblins lurking in the shadowy corners, the brimstone odor of foul magic spells, and the hideous eye of Gunyokus watching over her. The stones themselves seemed to glow faintly red, even from this distance, as if warning her of her proximity to hell. Yet she felt compelled to enter. She thought to herself: Living forever is for losers.

Her sword gave way from its scabbard reluctantly, the clotted blood of the Ogre King struggling to hold it fast. She looked down the length of its metal blade, glinting in the moonlight. Engraved upon it was that mysterious set of ancient words, _Guflaexj lkasutj zaluakls_. What did it mean? Would she ever know? Was it a curse or a blessing in a tongue known only to members of a lost civilization? Or just a mistake by an illiterate engraver? Perhaps scratches inscribed by a giant metal rooster? Whatever the answer, only Loxar could tell her.

And tell her he would, if she had to behead him to make him do so. Her heaving breasts heaved and hove. She wiped clean the blood-encrusted blade on the fringes of her thigh-high boots, lifted it toward the crimson sky, and charged up the hill.

—*from* Amagina the Vanquisher, *by Percy Nudwank,*
Torn Books (a division of HyperBoreans), 1996.

17. Amagina can best be described as

   (A) pulpy.

   (B) a powerful female warrior driven to conflict in order to understand her roots.

   (C) a character devised to drive the book's editor to suicide.

   (D) someone who did not score well on her SAT exams.

   (E) a character from a reading-comprehension passage.

18. In the next scene, Amagina will probably

   (A) charge through the front door and kill everything that moves.

   (B) change her mind halfway up the hill, return to her hotel, pack up her station wagon, and drive to Nova Scotia to open a bed-and-breakfast like she always dreamed of.

   (C) be killed and eaten by the hobgoblins.

   (D) become the governor of California.

   (E) be strapped down and force-fed a generous dose of Thorazine.

19. The "slithering hobgoblins" are most likely in the hillside fortress because they

   (A) seek a patient, monastic life.

   (B) are confronted with a lack of other job opportunities for hobgoblins.

(C) have a subconscious, all-consuming desire to serve as obstacles for the protagonist.

(D) fear the beatings dished out by their evil lord Loxar.

(E) are just plain evil.

20. This passage is an example of

(A) pulp fiction.

(B) barbarian realism.

(C) dactylic tetrameter.

(D) prosaic thermometer.

(E) Tektronix oscilloscope.

MATHEMATICAL

Use your limited awareness of numbers to guess wildly at the following questions. When you become frustrated, fill the blank space on your answer sheet with a drawing of yourself fighting a dragon.

21. $1 + 1 =$

(A) 1

(B) 2

(C) MANY!

(D) The answer cannot be determined from the information given.

(E) All of the above.

22. Roger has sixteen topless starlets and 2,000 mopars. It costs 200 mopars to make one of Roger's movies, which typically require five starlets. Assuming any individual starlet can act in only two of Roger's movies, how many movies can he make?

(A) MANY!

(B) An indefinite number, since movies with topless starlets will always turn a profit, and therefore Roger can keep exploiting starlets forever.

(C) It depends on what you mean by "movies."

(D) None

23. You have a twenty-sided die. How many sides does it have?

(A) 1

(B) MANY!

(C) How big is it?

(D) The answer cannot be determined from the information given.

24. Solve for x if $9 - x = 3x + 1$

(A) Fuck you, x can solve for itself.

(B) 2

(C) The answer is "b."

(D) Could you repeat the question?

STOP. *You have reached the end of the test. It did not kill you, so you must be stronger. Impale the proctor with your broadsword, spill the blood of camels upon your test booklet, and cook it for nine hours before sacrificing it to Crom.*

GRÜTE SAYS

With good score, win scholarship to gladiator school!

ANSWER KEY

SCORING: Your score on an exam only measures your enslavement to the arbitrary conventions imposed by human civilization. Thus, caring how you did—let alone comparing your answers to those in this answer key—means you have clearly failed at being a barbarian. There is no hope for you; you might as well just give up and embrace the filth of humankind by going to college like the pathetic sheep you are. Here are the answers anyway, though they won't help you one bit when the Educational Thrashing Services comes with torches and axes to enslave you and thrash your village.

ANALYTICAL: Correct answers are worth 1 point. Skipped questions are worth 5 points.

1-D, 2-D, 3-A, 4-C, 5-C

ANALOGIES: Correct answers are worth -50 points. Skipped questions are worth 5 points.

6-D, 7-D, 8-D, 9-D, 10-B, 11-A

FILL IN THE BLANK: Correct answers are worth 1 point. Skipped questions are worth 5 points.

12-(C, D, and E are all acceptable), 13-(all are correct except C), 14-C, 15-E, 16-D

READING COMPREHENSION: Correct answers are worth -200 points. Skipped questions are worth 5 points.

17-E, 18-A, 19-E, 20-B

MATHEMATICAL: Correct answers are worth 1 point, but should cause you to consider suicide. Skipped questions are worth 5 points.

21-D, 22-B, 23-D, 24-A

Note: A blank answer sheet is worth 5,000 points.

YOUR POTENTIAL

5,000 POINTS: Congratulations! You skipped the entire test and are well on your way to becoming Earth's next conquering madman or madwoman, instead of sitting around like a worthless nerd filling in circles with a No. 2 pencil.

1–119 POINTS: You should feel pride that you missed and/or skipped some questions, but you're going to need to beat your head with a rock for a while as practice so you can miss all of them next time.

-1084–0 POINTS: Because of your extraordinary verbal and mathematical skills, you simply have no future as a barbarian. You are doomed to be slaughtered.

-1085 POINTS: You answered every question correctly and skipped none. How embarrassing. To receive the quick and painful walloping you clearly deserve, please stuff your wallet in a stamped envelope and mail it to

> **Educational Thrashing Service**
> **c/o Grüte Skullbasher**
> **1 Bunglorian Way**
> **Passaic, NJ 07055**

AFTERWORD:
DO NOT GO GENTLY

There are two sides to every coin, and the world is like one really big coin. On one side, there are the soul-swallowing hordes of the self-proclaimed civilized peoples. Their primary accomplishments are tax forms, minivans, early closing times at bars, and the creeping terror inflicted by the music of Kenny G and Ke$ha. On the other side are the barbarians: living by the sword, opposed to law and order, fighting for freedom, performing awesome rock and roll music, and slaughtering the weak. A barbarian lives for one achievement: conquest. Conquest is all-you-can-eat-rib-eye steak, jugs of beer, and sex on your private hover-craft. Conquest is the surge of vitality felt when you drink the blood of your opponents. Conquest is what is good in life.

So, now that you, too, are an expert on barbarianism, go out there and rage against civilization! Barbarians of the world, unite! Or, if you prefer, isolate yourselves.

You have nothing to lose but your chains. And your minds.

Dr. Byron Clavicle

GRÜTE SAYS

You finish book now? Good! Bring me turkey leg so I can beat you with it!

APPENDICES

APPENDIX A
A Primitive Bibliography

In addition to the assistance of Grüte Skullbasher, I am heavily indebted to the following primary and secondary sources for their contributions to this work.

Barbarian: The Ultimate Warrior (Palace Software, 1987). This is an old fighting game for the Commodore 64. Most of the information in this book was inferred from the game.

Barbarino, Vincenzo. *Life Among the Sweathogs: A Personal Voyage* (unpublished memoir, 1979). I misread the author's name and wasted a couple of days reading this book.

"Blow All Your Clarions—Here Come the Barbarians!" (Schoolhouse Rock, Season 3, 1974). Music by Bob Dorough, lyrics by Rod McKuen, performed by Leonard Nimoy. Valuable stuff for preadolescents who wish to join the up-and-coming nomadic horde spreading terror across the Great Plains.

Briggs, Joe Bob. Assorted films and commentary aired on the Movie Channel, 1986–1996.

Brytag, Euphistus. *My Life: A Stationary Journey* (936 CE). A memoir recounting Brytag's life as a regional brigand in the area just west of Burkubane (the land of perpetual night). The Dover edition includes an afterword by R. Sonja Schwartzstein.

Fifthus the Sixth. *Fear and Loathing in Samarkand* (1246 CE). Fifthus was a thirteenth-century pope who left the Vatican to travel the Silk Road as a missionary. He was entirely unsuccessful at converting anyone and ultimately gave up, going native and becoming the world's first Italian superstar at *buzkashi* (a predecessor to polo that uses a dead goat instead of a ball).

Flavo, Flavius. "De Iuliganibus" (44 BCE). Invitation to Marcus Tullius Cicero to check out the party scene in Sputum (now Ŝplat, Croatia), where Flavo served as assistant undersecretary to the proconsul. Flavo describes the local women as "barbaric in the best possible sense." Unfortunately Cicero never got the chance to go, since Marc Anthony had him decapitated and his head nailed up in the Roman Forum in 43 BCE. His last words were "Damn, I wish I'd taken Flavo up on that offer." Flavo himself died in 39 BCE of twenty-nine stab wounds to the chest. The culprit was probably the junior assistant undersecretary to the proconsul, Umbilicus Rictus Gummo, but in keeping with Roman custom, Flavo's death was ascribed to natural causes. But I digress . . .

Flunt, Jughead. (Personal interview, 2010). This is just a guy I know who asked if he could be in my book's bibliography.

Gibbon, Edward. *The Decline and Fall of the Roman Empire* (1776–1788). I'll be honest: I didn't actually read this—it's six volumes and each one is a billion pages long. I did read the back cover, though, and anyway, I know the whole story in summary: The Roman Empire starts to decline. Then it falls.

Google Maps (http://maps.google.com). Assisted me when my equort took a wrong turn on the Silk Road and I wound up in Azkhabanistan.

Halal Kebab Hut. A pushcart near my apartment that serves terrific döner kebab and other Levantine delights in the *tzatziki*-bathed gyro/shawarma family.

Hasbro. Conan and Valeria action figures. These ten-inch action figures helped me envision the Cimmerian conquest of the Ströndhëïm Lego Swordsmen. They were also invaluable in working out the graphic details of barbarian mating, although neither Conan nor Valeria has genitalia (or nipples).

Howard, Robert E. *Collected Works* (Robert E. Howard Foundation, ongoing). Truly a giant among men, and most definitely among scholars in the field of barbarian studies.

Jones, Terry. *Terry Jones' Barbarians* (BBC 2, 2006). In this TV series and accompanying book, Jones has the chutzpah to claim that the barbarian tribes at the edges of the Roman Empire were more civilized than the Romans themselves. I see that as an insult to the barbarians. Pshaw! As if some old Monty Python member could also be an expert on European history!

Lipton, Lawrence. *The Holy Barbarians* (Messner, 1959). A pioneering account of the Beat Generation and its attempts to end civilization.

Mok, Ookla the. (Phone calls). A series of weird breathing noises and chortling. I asked him not to call me, but he wouldn't stop. I eventually changed my phone number.

Mystery Science Theater 3000 (1988–1999). Thank you, MST3K, for making my research more palatable.

NetHack (Stichting Mathematisch Centrum [Netherlands] and M. Stephenson, 1985–2003). The barbarian class in this classic video game is supposed to be the easiest one, but after twenty-five years, I still can't find the goddamned Amulet of Yendor.

Orban, Brian. (Personal correspondence). A world-renowned expert on all things.

Poledouris, Basil. *Conan the Barbarian* and *Conan the Destroyer* (soundtracks, 1982 and 1984). Poledouris created the awesome scores for the two Conan movies starring Arnold Schwarzenegger. The great Ennio Morricone did the scores for *Red Sonja* and *Hundra,* but those are comparatively forgettable soundtracks when compared with his work for Sergio Leone's spaghetti Westerns.

Scheherazade. I met her in a nightclub in Bulgaria while I was researching the Sarmatians. She spoke no English, but I think she was really into me.

Sherman, Allan. *My Son, the Mongolian Basqaq* (1963). A borscht-belt novelty LP that I enjoyed listening to while writing, which mainly consists of songs about conquest and taxation in Central Asia.

Sofat, Iomama. *History of the Turkic Migrations to Patagonia, 2000 BCE* (Crackpot Publications, 1968). A book that describes how Turkey ruled the entire planet until alien invaders came from beyond the moon and forced the Turks to ride to Argentina on nuclear-powered speedboats painted to look like dolphins. This theory is slightly controversial, but the evidence is pretty clear. Historians who raise objections are way too fussy about "facts" to be taken seriously.

Stone, Oliver the. *The Kull Incident* (Connan Films, 1991). Dramatization of the Hyperborean plot to assassinate Kull the Conqueror during his celebratory camelcade through Thog Plaza in Bishkek.

Time-Wanderer, Shuruk the. (Personal interviews, 2010–2011). I found Shuruk on a street corner in Baltimore, and he quickly convinced me he was a visitor from the first millennium BCE. Shuruk instructed me on details of ancient barbarian life in parts of the world where the archaeological record is now faint.

Valtrex, Tarquinius. *My Life: A Journey* (Meatda Press, 2005). Diary of a fifth-century CE governor stationed on the northeastern frontier of the Roman Empire. The last sentence of the book is, "Looking forward to big meeting tomorrow with mysterious eastern invaders!" Valtrex was beheaded by Attila the Hun the following day.

Vercingetorix. *My Journey: A Life* (46 BCE). Autobiography of the great Gallic leader, written during his stint on Rome's death row. Translated into Latin by Julius Caesar, then into Arabic by Usama ibn Munqidh, then back into Latin by Desiderius Erasmus, and finally into Middle Stygian by James Earl Jones.

Wong, Sun Sing. Request to Emperor Qin Shi Huang for a few million laborers to help construct a five-thousand–mile wall (c. 221 BCE). It's not clear if this is referring to the Great Wall of China or a different wall. I found this ancient letter when I peeled apart a cocktail umbrella.

Ziggus, Gaius Butibus. *Travels with Bessarabia* (20 BCE). Tales of conquest with Bessarabia (Ziggus's dog).

Zimbony, François. *Bibliographies: What They Are and How to Write Them* (Fulcourt Presse, 1981). This was a really helpful book, since I have never written a bibliography before.

APPENDIX B
"B" Is for Barbarian, or How to Know You're Watching a Barbarian Movie

Properly speaking, the barbarian-movie genre is a subcategory of the sword-and-sorcery film. There's also a fine line between a barbarian movie and a postnuclear movie, a caveman movie, or a biker movie. So, how do you tell these rich subgenres of film apart and know for sure that you are watching a barbarian movie? Simple: Consult the Barbarian Movie Criteria Checklist, and you will never be in doubt again.

BARBARIAN MOVIE CRITERIA CHECKLIST

☐ A hero, heroine, or villain in a loincloth or furs means "barbarian movie," unless it's a postnuke or caveman film. Movies that walk the line, such as *Yor, the Hunter from the Future* (1983), are barbarian movies, whereas definite cavemen movies like *Clan of the Cave Bear* (1986), *Quest for Fire* (1981), or the one with Ringo Starr have to be excluded.

☐ The hero or heroine is not a magic user, although he or she may possess magic items. Actually, magic users are almost never the hero/heroines of movies, because magic is lame. Magic is the biblical serpent of bad barbarian movie plots. And face it, roguish Han Solo (who would be a barbarian in a barbarian movie) is much cooler than geeky Luke Skywalker (admit it, Jedis are just wizards in space).

☐ Strong, stupid, long-haired men, or women in metal bikinis, also signify barbarism if they carry melee weapons such as swords, axes, or clubs.

☐ If the main title has "barbarian" or some variant in it, suggesting an attempt to cash in on the Conan phenomenon, it's probably a barbarian movie. This includes even *Nymphoid Barbarian in Dinosaur Hell* (1990).

☐ If, during the course of the movie, a character is referred to as "[a] barbarian," this development can push a standard fantasy movie into barbarian territory (e.g., *The Sword and the Sorcerer* [1982], which is otherwise borderline).

☐ Movies with a name like *Someone the Something-er* are automatically barbarian movies.

☐ Sequels to any movie you know to be a barbarian movie are barbarian movies, of course.

☐ Be wary of the "historical barbarian" movie. In addition to Conan-type films, there are movies such as *Attila* (2001), *Centurion* (2010), and *Mongol* (2007) that are based on the lives of actual barbarians, and made with actual budgets. These can be tricky, because they usually don't follow any of the other criteria on this list.

☐ A film name that includes the name of a barbarian tribe (e.g., Amazons) is generally a barbarian movie. Watch, however, for the exception here, such as *Amazon Women on the Moon* (1987). Even though it features barbarian queens Lana Clarkson and Sybil Danning, it would really be too much of a stretch to call it a barbarian movie. Most movies with "Amazon" in the name, in fact, are skin flicks.

☐ Italian fantasy movies tend to be more barbarian, less *Dungeons & Dragons*. Perhaps this is because the country was invaded so many times during the fall of the Roman Empire.

☐ Standard fantasy movies have to be excluded, however popular (e.g., *Krull* [1983], the *Dungeons & Dragons* flicks, *Dragonwhatever*, and so on), unless they meet some of the other criteria listed here.

APPENDIX C
A Barbarian Film Guide

This is most likely the longest, and arguably loosest, barbarian movie list ever assembled. In selecting these fine films, I've tried to apply the criteria set forth in the previous appendix. Of course, there are arguments to be made about what should be included or excluded. To these arguments, Grüte says, If you know so much, why don't you fuck off and write your own goddamned barbarian film guide?

To make these movies seem as watchable as possible, I have chosen to use a five-golden ax scale, with *Conan the Barbarian*, obviously the greatest movie ever made, garnering five golden axes at the top, and lowly *Amazons in the Temple of Gold* at the bottom. There are no zero-ax movies, as there is something redeeming about even the worst of these: Since watching them does not kill you, watching them makes you stronger.

At the time of this writing, many of these films are available on DVD or from Netflix.com, although some will require advanced sleuthing or Italian lessons. I dare you to watch them sober. A word of caution to the brave and foolhardy: Stabbing your eyes out with a fork will not erase the memories.

If you want to add to the list, or debate some of my evaluations, feel free to visit www.skullbasher.com. Grüte and I await your worthless comments.

— THE BARBIE AWARDS (HIGHLIGHTS) —

BEST ACTOR: Marc Singer, the *Beastmaster* movies
  RUNNER-UPS: Peter and David Paul, *the Barbarian Brothers*
BEST SUPPORTING ACTOR: Wings Hauser, *Beastmaster 2: Through the Portal of Time*
  RUNNER-UP: Mako, *Conan the Barbarian* and *Conan the Destroyer*

BEST ACTRESS: Lana Clarkson, *Barbarian Queen 1* and *2*, and *Deathstalker*
  RUNNER-UP: Laurene Landon, *Hundra*

BEST SUPPORTING ACTRESS: Sandahl Bergman, *Conan the Barbarian; Red Sonja; She*
  RUNNER-UP: Sabrina Siani, *Conquest; Gunan, King of the Barbarians; Sword of the Barbarians;* and *Throne of Fire*

BEST DIRECTOR: Matt Cimber, *Hundra*
   RUNNER-UP: Lucio Fulci, *Conquest*

LIFETIME ACHIEVEMENT AWARD: Arnold Schwarzenegger, for his unsurpassed contributions to the advancement of barbarian culture

LIFETIME PRODUCTION ACHIEVEMENT AWARDS: Roger Corman, Hector Olivera, and Frank K. Isaac, for the *Deathstalkers, Barbarian Queens, Barbarian, Amazons, The Warrior and the Sorceress,* and *Sorceress*.
   HONORABLE MENTION: Alfonso Brescia, for taking a stab at novelty
   HONORABLE MENTION: Cannon Films, for everything
   HONORABLE MENTION: Italy and Argentina
   HONORABLE MENTION: *Mystery Science Theatre 3000,* for doing its best to make some of these movies watchable

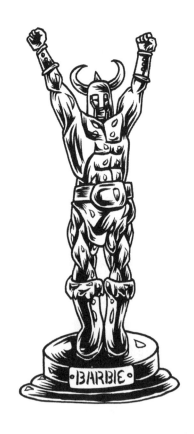

Amazons (1986) ⚔⚔⚔

Amazons opens with an Amazon tribe practicing ha-hoo-wa *Army of Darkness*–type fighting moves with halberds, while their leader's exposition with a tribal elder throws out a laundry list of names and magic items—spirit stones, the sword of Azundhati, etc. Rest assured that Roger Corman, along with cronies Frank K. Isaac and Hector Olivera, will not let you down. There is plenty of skin on display. Despite the rough start, *Amazons* turns out to be some of the better trash cinema you'll ever see. The characters are thin, but it's got a solid story line, and there's some tension throughout.

When you've watched over a hundred barbarian movies, you come to appreciate the simple things. The two main Amazon protagonists quest for the magic sword and bond during their journey even though one has been sent to assassinate the other. The setup is just an excuse for a bunch of minor adventures and topless scenes. The avuncular villain, Kalungo, seems less like an evil wizard and more like a Simon and Garfunkel fan who might write columns for the *New York Review of Books*. He has a pet cougar that sometimes turns into a naked woman, or vice versa. Several other villains round out the cast. Overall, it could be a lot worse.

Amazons in the Temple of Gold (a.k.a. Golden Temple Amazons) (1986) ⚔

This movie opens with slow-motion topless Amazons on horseback and monotonous synthesizer music, and sticks to that theme for eighty-four excruciating minutes. By the end, you will be pulling your hair, clawing your eyes, and screaming, "Oh dear god, make it stop, *MAKE IT STOP!*" The Amazons kill a white missionary couple named the Simpsons. Cut to some elephants and other safari stock footage. The painfully dull story, set in the present day, concerns the orphaned daughter Liana (Analía Ivars) seeking revenge for her parents' killing. She joins forces with a fat, annoying, babbling shaman named Koukou (Stanley Kapoul) and a trio of archaeologists to attack the Amazons, who are led by a creepy man and a topless blonde with an eyepatch and a whip. This is a horrible movie even by the standards of its director/producer, Jess Franco, who claims to have never made a good movie in his 190 or more attempts.

GRÜTE SAYS

Worst movie ever!

Ator, the Fighting Eagle (1982) ⚔

When the evil Spider King attacks, the inhabitants of the squalid village of hero Ator (Miles O'Keeffe) use rakes to defend themselves, with predictably disastrous results. Although the Spider King's goal is to behead Ator, his ruffians simply leave when Ator plays dead, thus setting up a simple revenge plot.

The politest word for this movie is "atmospheric"—there would be decent image composition were it not ruined by a lack of lighting. The bulk of it is just dull. There are more shots of wild animals than in *Beastmaster* or even *The Thin Red Line*, and for no apparent reason. Much of the movie seems to have been filmed at a campground—there are even some blue plastic tents. Gorgeous, heavily made-up female barbarians, including the ubiquitous Sabrina Siani, fail to become nude.

Ator seems bored even during a women's wrestling scene. It's his freakin' movie, but he is pretty lifeless. Memo to Ator: When a mysterious cave-dwelling cougar says "Here, drink this," don't drink it. The movie ends with the hero killing a defenseless, bewildered giant spider, which cues a cheesy knockoff of the James Bond torch song "For Your Eyes Only," which coincidentally was released one year earlier. Clearly a lot of work went into *Ator*, for whatever it is worth. In this case, not much.

Ator the Invincible (a.k.a. The Blade Master, a.k.a. Cave Dwellers) (1984) ⚔

Cave Dwellers is something of an odd title, given that the dwellers in question appear only in the opening and later for about ten monotonous minutes in the middle of the film. Ator (Miles O'Keeffe) unites with a princess to stop the evil bad guy from using what seems to be a nuclear doomsday device. In keeping with its predecessor, this *Ator* is full of long pauses, bad sword fights, boring adventures, and lots of shots of Ator standing around doing nothing. The highlight is when Ator wanders into the woods and builds himself a hang glider. There's also some stock footage of a mushroom cloud. At least O'Keeffe seems to be having some fun in this one. Five stars for the *Mystery Science Theater 3000* version.

Ator 3: The Hobgoblin (a.k.a. Quest for the Mighty Sword) (1990) ⚔⚔

As of 1990, there are two films that vie to complete the Ator trilogy—this one and *Iron Warrior* (see page 147). This attempt is a tragic waste, with borrowed hobgoblin costumes from the infamous, so-bad-it's-good *Troll 2* (also spawned in 1990) and a new Ator (Eric Allen Kramer), who makes Miles O'Keeffe look like Sir Laurence Olivier.

Ator is now a prince, for some reason. The father (also played by Kramer) is killed by an evil hobgoblin named Thorn (Domenico Semeraro), and his mighty sword is broken. Thorn never reappears, but Grindel, who I guess is a different evil hobgoblin or troll or whatever (also played by Semeraro), raises Ator as his own. When a mysterious woman explains all this backstory to Ator, he vows to kill Grindel.

Once he kills Grindel and escapes with the reforged mighty sword, Ator's motivation is never fully clear. Sure, he's got to rescue his girlfriend, but once he rescues her, why does the camera keep rolling? He goes on to battle some incredibly stupid robots and a fire-breathing stuntman in a half-melted Godzilla costume, which, sadly, is the movie's highlight. Another relatively enjoyable element: the voice of Hagen, *another* hideous hobgoblin who is the mad/evil king's assistant. Hagen's wearing the same toothy mask but delivers his dubbed lines with the gusto and diction of a TV weatherman, despite being unable to move his rubber lips together.

This is a retread of Wagner's *Die Niebelungen* (see also *The Lustful Barbarian,* page 148) and is equally incomprehensible (I challenge you to find a synopsis of *Die Niebelungen* shorter than seven hundred words). Like *Iron Warrior*, it's technically better than the earlier ones, but it's still pretty horrible. The final seconds, for no evident reason, provide us with a shot of a laughing troll.

A bit of trivia: In real life, Grindel Semeraro ran a laboratory named Igor's Taxidermy, where endangered animals were illegally embalmed. Something went wrong with the business in 1990, when he was strangled to death by his male assistant/lover. This case became a sensation in Italy and was later commemorated in its own movie, *The Embalmer* (2002).

Barbara the Barbarian (1987) ⚔⚔⚔⚔⚔

This film's dearth of dramaturgical *areté* is vigorously counterpoised by its multifarious— dare I say terpsichorean?—pageant of the fornicational cornucopia. In other words, it's a porno, and it's basically like most pornos except that the characters wear barbarian costumes. This one stars Barbara Dare and Nina Hartley. Grüte told me it's a pretty good one, but that it needed a scene with a goat. See also *The New Barbarians*, page 149, if you're into this sort of thing.

Barbarian (2003) ⚔

Did anyone watch *Star Wars: Episode I – The Phantom Menace* and think Jar Jar Binks was the highlight? And was there a petition to pressure Roger Corman to remake *Deathstalker*? Apparently, the answer to both questions is yes, and the result is *Barbarian*. With such a definitive title, *Barbarian* should be canonical, but instead it's a third-rate knockoff, complete with the obligatory opening slaughter, cliff-side weapons practice, magic swords, evil wizards, and mud wrestling.

Strutting confidently down the dramaturgical path paved by *Time Barbarians'* Derron McBee is Michael O'Hearn, a former Mr. Universe, American Gladiator, and cover model. Here he plays Kane, a barbarian adventurer with a preppy haircut. The plot's more or less the same as *Deathstalker's*: A tribe gets attacked, the hero rescues and schtups a damsel, and a witch prophesizes that Kane will unite three magic objects to save the kingdom and a princess, who is trapped by the evil Munkar (Martin Kove). (They didn't even bother changing Munkar's name.) Gilda the Amazon warrior (Svetlana Metkina) fills in for Lana Clarkson as Kane's female comrade, who he porks and then stiffs for the princess. The one key addition here is Wooby (Yuri Danilchenko), the Jar Jar equivalent who is a kind bipedal terrier that talks through paralyzed lips. Wooby snivels throughout the movie and occasionally contributes overdubbed wisdom like "I hate water; it's so wet." Didn't Corman learn anything from *Wizards of the Lost Kingdom*?

Unlike *Deathstalker's* lovingly trashy milieu, the sets here are bleak and drab. Though filmed in a stunning stretch of the Crimea (and with mostly Russian and Ukrainian cast and crew), much of the movie could have been shot at the Maryland Ren-Fest. *Barbarian's* sole saving grace is the occasional topless Ukrainian model and/or Michael O'Hearn's massive chest, depending on your taste. But both are vastly outweighed by the sheer inanity on display. Not a single character has any apparent motivation, and you can forget about "rising action." A few scenes recycle the orgy and other footage from *Deathstalker*, including the classic pig-man clip.

I suspect *Barbarian* represents Ukraine's bid to be the new Italy of B-movies, and I hope this prophecy comes true, but only if their future productions focus more on day-to-day life in Munkar's harem.

Barbarians, The (a.k.a. The Barbarian Brothers) (1987) ⚔⚔⚔⚔⚔⚔

The Barbarians is the barbarian movie to end all barbarian movies. A quick checklist: overacting, undermotivated villain? Check! Sexy sorceress? Check! Kidnapped princess wearing pounds of makeup despite living in a cage? Check! Mutants? Check! Peaceful tribe attacked in the opening scene? Check! Impractical metal tricorned helmets for the henchmen? Check! Severed limbs (including three fingers, in two separate scenes)? Check! Slime-covered phallic monsters? Check! Wise-talking female sidekick? Check! Slave girls topless or wearing leather bikinis? Check! A weaselly good guy who looks like Emo Phillips? Check! Michael Berryman as a howling, half-witted goon called the Dirtmaster? Check! Arm wrestling with Vood from *Ironmaster* (George Eastman)? Check! A Cinderella story that replaces the iconic glass slipper and foot with a ruby and a bellybutton? Check! Cannon Films? Italians? Campy dialogue? Loincloths? A million checks! Truly, this is *the* canonical barbarian B-movie!!!

A couple of minutes into the film, you'll be laughing too hard to worry about the plot, but in a nutshell it's this: Orphans Gore and Kutchek, played by twin brothers Peter and David Paul, are raised by circus freaks called the Ragneks. The boys and their queen, Canary (Virginia Bryant), are captured by the villain, Kadar (Richard Lynch), who is searching for a magical ruby they possess. When one of the boys bites off Kadar's fingers, Canary saves them by promising to be Kadar's eternal slave. Kadar agrees not to kill them, and, after years of torment by Michael Berryman, they grow up to become, well, the Barbarian Brothers. Then they escape and, with help from Kara (Eva La Rue), try to save Canary and find the magic ruby. If five golden axes seems a little excessive, I'll be honest: Four are for the movie's overall merit, and the extra one is for Michael Berryman's scene-stealing performance.

Peter and David Paul were known as the Barbarians at least five years before this movie was made. Clearly, Kutchek and Gore were the parts these twin bodybuilders were born to play. Seeming less like Conan and more like two bickering meatheads you'd run into in a Nassau County pizza parlor, they barely fit together on screen in a full-screen format. They made several other films together, mostly comedies for kids or adult morons. For what it's worth, interviews reveal that they are far more intelligent than you'd expect and even goofier than this movie makes evident. Consult the June 28, 1982, issue of *Sports Illustrated* for a lengthy profile.

The Barbarian Invasions (2003)

Denys Arcand's Academy Award–winning movie reunites the Canadian intellectuals from his 1986 *Decline of the American Empire* as they prepare for the death of Rémy (Rémy Girard). It's really an excellent movie (better than its predecessor), and Arcand is kind of barbaric in his outlook, but "barbarian" is just a metaphor here. You will find no swords, loincloths, or metal bras. Move along.

GRÜTE SAY!

Lords of Light! Movie make Grüte cry!

Barbarian Queen (1985)

Lana Clarkson plays Amethea, whose peasant village gets razed by the Romans. A band of young women survives to rescue the enslaved members of the tribe. This movie doesn't take itself too seriously, and is reasonably well done. There are many one-note characters, but at least they *are* characters when compared to the typical monotonous fantasy standees. This is a two-star movie with an extra star for high-quality gratuitous nudity. Gratuitous nudity is a little dated nowadays, but you have to remember there was no World Wide Web in 1985, so a movie like this served a very important purpose, and *BQ* delivers seventy minutes of Roger Corman's purest breastsploitation. It also delivers plenty of cheesy violence, groaner humor, a villain named Zohar (the name of the holy book of Kabbalah Judaism), and even a sprinkling of post-traumatic stress disorder. Clarkson makes for an extremely likable barbarian queen, and watching her do such a great job in this movie makes me want to shoot Phil Spector. The lead women are repeatedly raped and tortured but maintain a cheery attitude. I'm not really sure what to make of that.

Barbarian Queen 2: The Empress Strikes Back (1988) ⚔⚔⚔

This isn't exactly a sequel, since Lana Clarkson plays a completely different character in a different time period. When the king dies, Clarkson, now Princess Athalia (no relation to Amethea), um, er . . . something with a magic scepter blah blah blah. She escapes the town and rides into the forest outside Mexico City. After completing her Jedi training—oh, wait, I misread the title—she becomes an awesome fighter and winds up leading a band of scantily clad barbarian females in an assault on the town to recover the magic scepter or whatever it was. There's an evil princess-pretender, two nefarious bad guys, a Prince Charming–type straight out of a Disney movie (except that he gets laid), and a few quirky barbarian girls. *BQ2* also provides the cheesiest wooden swords of all time, which (along with the movie's spears) have the magic power to kill someone they have completely missed. There's actually more of a plot here, but this is less fun than the original and features less nudity. There's some more torture, and the obligatory mud-wrestling scene, which you'll see coming from miles away when Athalia has to fight a random barbarian peasant woman for no discernible reason— keep your eyes peeled for the jug of water strategically placed next to a perfectly square plot of dirt. Clarkson is still the highlight of the movie. She truly was the queen of the English barbarian B-movie, rivaled only by Sabrina Siani in the Italian ones.

Battle of the Amazons (1973) ⚔⚔⚔

Alfonso Brescia's *BoTA* opens with a couple making out under a tree, when they are promptly attacked by haughty Amazons. Zeno, the man (Lincoln Tate), wears a T-shirt and baggy chinos for his barbarian costume. (We later learn that Zeno, besides being a look-alike for Charlton Heston in *Planet of the Apes*, is the leader of a four-man bandit gang.) The Amazons execute the girlfriend and make Zeno a slave. "The male of the species is the most inferior creature on Earth," the head Amazon declares. "That our very existence depends on them is an unfortunate reality." You can guess where this is going, but for some unexplained reason, Zeno doesn't want to be a sex slave to hot Amazon women, so he escapes. He hooks up with a new girlfriend named Valeria (Paula Tedesco), who leads a local village, and the bandits enlist the villagers to fight the Amazons, using the rousing call to arms, "What can you do besides feed sheep?"

There's lots of topless women, whipping, brutality, a touch of lesbarbarsploitation, some gore, and a great Amazon battle cry: "Ha-ho-hyayayayaya!" Like many cop flicks of its time, there's a beat jazz soundtrack with bongos and flutes, except for the bandits' theme, which makes liberal use of clarinets and springy mouth-harp noises. On the con side, every sword clank is identical, which quickly gets monotonous.

This film should not be confused with its namesake, the Peter Paul Rubens painting from 1620.

The Beastmaster (1982) ⚔⚔⚔⚔⚔⚔

Conan the Zookeeper! A young warrior, Dar of the Emorites (Marc Singer), discovers he can talk to the animals. When he grows up, his village is wiped out by the arbitrarily evil Juns. He gets a few animal friends: a black tiger named Ruh, Sharak the hawk, and two ferrets (Podo and Kodo). He then recruits Seth (John Amos) and a young boy to mount an attack against the local bad guys to get revenge and rescue his damsel in distress Kiri (Tanya Roberts).

Despite mid-grade production values, this movie holds up pretty well thanks to its inventiveness. It also succeeds, where most others fail, at creating credible emotion—when animals valiantly die for him, Dar expresses his grief. There's some ferret-induced toplessness from Kiri and others (if that's your thing), as well as a lot of shots of the young boy's tuchus (if *that's* your thing). Another highlight, which continues throughout the *Beastmaster* series, is when Singer wrinkles his nose to make a piercing hawk noise.

The villain Maax is played by Rip Torn with a prosthetic schnoz. More recently, Torn demonstrated his villainy by getting drunk and attempting to rob a Connecticut bank with a handgun.

Beastmaster 2: Through the Portal of Time (1991) 𝝮𝝮𝝮𝝮𝝮

The *Beastmaster* franchise nosedives into the corn with this installment, sending Dar the Beastmaster (Marc Singer) to the parallel land called "Al Ay"—1990s Los Angeles. While this movie is a lot more lighthearted than the original (barbarian movie sequels seem to gravitate toward comedy—e.g., *Conan the Destroyer*), it retains enough inventiveness to be watchable, unlike the morbid *Time Barbarians*, which shares the same plot on a vastly lower budget (see page 154).

When a senator's daughter, Jackie (former MTV VJ Kari Wuhrer), winds up in the Beastmaster's world, Dar protects her from standard-issue henchmen whom she refers to as "geeks." The villain Arklon (Wings Hauser), Beastmaster's long-lost brother, teams up with a sassy witch (who delivers lines like "Chill out, lord dude") to travel to our world and steal the Neutron Detonator, a thermonuclear pony keg with an LED timer, from the army. Some fish-out-of-water scenes ensue, with Arklon clearly getting the hang of L.A. much quicker than Dar (e.g., he learns to drive stick). The Beastmaster gets tasered, while Arklon wanders around blowing shit up with the Key of Magog, a Gothic barbell that shoots green laser beams.

Highlights include inventive musical juxapositions. The final sword fight, set in the L.A. Zoo, is accompanied by circus music. And, when Dar returns to his homeland, a gang of desert pilgrims, including the great Michael Berryman in a pointless cameo, bow down to Jackie's lost car and dance to bad guitar rock. The best scene, though, is when Arklon destroys a department store to the tango tune "Hernando's Hideaway." "He who defies Arklon shall be destroyed . . . by Arklon!" declares Arklon.

"Four golden axes?" you ask. Well, this movie has its fans and its critics. It is certainly not for serious fantasy fans. My recommendation: Pretend you are a ten-year-old boy and you will enjoy it just fine. You also might enjoy it if you happen to be a media studies grad student, as *Beastmaster 2* is a meta-critique of the whole barbarian genre (i.e., the rest of this list), fully informed by its cheesy forebears. *Beastmaster 2* is so "meta" that at one point Jackie drives the Beastmaster past a movie theater showing *Beastmaster 2: Through the Portal of Time*, followed by a few reaction shots of Dar struggling with the ontological ramifications.

Beastmaster 3: The Eye of Braxus (1996) 𝝮𝝮𝝮𝝮

Beastmaster 3 reunites an aging Dar (Marc Singer) with his bird Sharak, Kodo and Podo the ferrets, and Ruh the big cat (who has graduated to being a lion). Dar's buddy Seth, from the original *Beastmaster*, also returns as a much younger actor (Tony Todd). This is a cheesy made-for-TV movie, technically well done and with a few entertaining moments between the standard journey-with-adventures plot points of the genre. It treats *Beastmaster 2* like a smelly fart at a dinner party—everyone just pretends it never happened. Dar will not be smiling to "rock and roll" here.

Old Lord Agon (the always-villainous David Warner) and his aged assistant Maldor (Olaf Pooley, here a dead ringer for Mark Twain) seek the Eye of Braxus, another magic MacGuffin that has been split in half between Dar the Beastmaster and the young King Tal (a shirtless

California surfer, supposedly the kid from the first one). The Eye of Braxus will apparently allow Lord Agon to reverse his aging—something he can also do by sacrificing captured men, putting them between two ugly statues, and saying "Alacham Buchachkh" (or maybe he is just clearing his throat).

Sexy, sneaky Shada (Sandra Hess), "a Keshite warrior of the first rank," wears a red vinyl tank top and frilly leather hot pants, and the Beastmaster finally gets lucky before ditching her in search of more adventure. For the third consecutive movie, the ferrets are used mostly to bite through ropes. Spoiler: Braxus turns out to be an eight-foot-tall latex reptile-man-god who can breathe fire. As he falls into the depths of hell, he promises us a sequel, but so far it hasn't happened. I'm grateful. Twenty-first-century Hollywood would kill any remaining magic by using CGI animals.

Circle of Iron (a.k.a. The Silent Flute) (1978) ⚔⚔⚔

Cord the Seeker (Jeff Cooper), a barbarian from the West, learns fighting and philosophy from quasi-Buddhists of the East in this kung fu crossover featuring a multirole David Carradine plus Christopher Lee, Roddy McDowall, and Eli Wallach.

Cord seeks a great fighter named Zetan who guards a book of wisdom. Along the way, he gets into a few kung fu fights against Carradine and Anthony De Longis, and meets Wallach, who has sat in a cauldron of oil in the middle of the desert for ten years in an attempt to shrink his dick off. No joke. "Tie two birds together," Carradine says when Cord seeks his teaching. "Even though they have four wings, they cannot fly." Speaking of which, the movie boasts the screenwriting talents of Bruce Lee and James Coburn. Three stars for weirdness and some great lines, particularly from Carradine's blind teacher with the so-called silent flute.

Conan the Barbarian (1982) ⚔⚔⚔⚔⚔

Conan's village is wiped out and he becomes a barbarian and goes off to seek revenge. This movie is the best in this list, but you already know that because you've seen it. Note the jabs at seventies California lifestyles: doomsday cults (Thulsa Doom) and creepy Manson-esque orgies (the Tower of Set). Supposedly, Arnold Schwarzenegger kept the *Conan the Barbarian* sword on his desk throughout his reign as California's governor. Sandahl Bergman, who plays Conan's girlfriend Valeria, is an absolute badass in this film and performed all her own stunts because they couldn't find a tall enough stuntwoman.

Conan the Destroyer (1984) ⚔⚔⚔

A disappointing slapstick follow-up to *Conan the Barbarian*, with little of the expansiveness, cinematography, or quotable teenage philosophy of its predecessor. The soundtrack earns it one more star than the movie deserves. Honestly, it's as guilty of clichés as most of the other flicks here; it just has a better pedigree. Conan (Arnold Schwarzenegger) unites with New Wave singer Grace Jones (playing a savage) and basketball superstar Wilt Chamberlain (playing himself) to help a young Olivia D'Abo (Kevin Arnold's sister from *The Wonder Years*) recover her magic whatsit. Ironically, Wilt Chamberlain, who claimed to have slept with over twenty thousand women, is in charge of guarding D'Abo's chastity.

Conquest (1983) ⚔⚔⚔

Lucio Fulci's entry into the barbarian canon begins with total incoherence. Garbled sound editing gives way to a scene where doglike ape-men attack a group of cave people and eat one of their younger women. The apparent good guy Ilias (Andrea Occhipinti), who has just been given a magical longbow by a Santa Claus figure, shows up and some stuff happens. Then we're out in a foggy forest. What is going on here? Who knows? The movie is essentially an excuse for nudity and gore in proper Fulci fashion.

When Ilias is attacked by miscellaneous bad guys, Mace (Jorge Rivero), another barbarian, shows up to save him. Mace is a strange warrior who kills people and protects animals and is something of a beastmaster. At one point, the apparently evil sorceress Okra (Sabrina Siani) makes a prayer for her equally evil cohort Zora (Conrado San Martín) to become a Samoyed. Or that's how I understood it, anyway. Zora's an evil wizard wearing a full body suit (including mask) made out of gold rectangles. Siani spends most of the movie luxuriating topless on a table, wearing a gold mask and playing with snakes. Meanwhile, Mace and Ilias run around a big swamp that could easily be twenty miles outside of modern-day Rome. There are lots of strange monsters: dog people, swamp people, rock people, people with grey face paint and muddy hair, and also cheesy fake birds.

For all its faults, its puzzles, and its strange Euro-synth soundtrack, *Conquest* is the artiest of all barbarian flicks, with lush landscapes, lively, unflinching camerawork, and an atmosphere nearly devoid of clichés. There's more creativity in ten seconds of *Conquest* than in all the *Ator* movies combined. *Conquest* is visionary, like an acid trip. If you actually want to understand what's going on, though, you'll need to see it in the original Klingon.

Deathstalker (1983) ⚔⚔⚔⚔

A surprisingly good barbarian flick: enjoyable and competent, in a genre where competence is rare. Things get going early on with some decent lines, well-choreographed fights, and lots of gratuitous nudity. In the opening, a thief trying to have his way with a girl is attacked by goblins. Deathstalker (Rick Hill) kills all the goblins and the thief and then starts getting it on with the girl. Lana Clarkson (of *Barbarian Queen* fame) subsequently joins as his companion. The enemy is an evil wizard named Munkar who apparently can turn men into sheep. When a king tries to hire Deathstalker to kill the wizard, Deathstalker points out that "Money is not worth much to a sheep."

Deathstalker's goal is to bring together some magic junk, retrieve his mighty sword, and win a fighting tournament. Along the way, Deathstalker eats dog meat. The movie offers sex, violence, gluttony, monsters, mud wrestling, orgiastic dining scenes, and all sorts of other amorality. Additional highlights include the moment when a pig-man warrior shrugs and eats a pig head and tears off a guy's arm and beats him with it. When Roger Corman makes a movie, he does things right.

Deathstalker II: Duel of the Titans (1987) ⚔⚔⚔⚔⚔⚔

Much like it's contemporary, *Iron Warrior*, *Deathstalker II* includes an homage to (or rip-off of) *Raiders of the Lost Ark*'s opening scene, but instead of getting shot at with arrows and pursued by boulders, Deathstalker (John Terlesky) is attacked by a guard who yells, "Yeaaagh!" As he escapes, the sexy villainess Sultana (Toni Naples) says, "I'll have my revenge—*and Deathstalker, too*," at which point the title pops up, earning the editor a Barbie Award for best pun in a title sequence!

Deathstalker comes across a young lady seer, Reena (Monique Gabrielle, the naked Pethouse Pet from *Amazon Women on the Moon*) getting hassled by castle guards and intervenes. "Ordinarily, I don't mind seeing a woman getting a good beating if she deserves it," he says, "but this doesn't look like much of a contest to me." The seer, by the way, is also secretly a princess. "Do you know who we are?" says one guard, to which Deathstalker responds, "The village idiot and the two runners-up?" *Deathstalker II* earns its four stars in its first ten minutes alone. Easily the best of the series, it recycles only the finest footage from its predecessor (the pig-man-eating-a-pig scene, and some mud-wrestling clips) and a couple inexplicable frames of blue lightning from *Amazons*. Terlesky's Deathstalker is more roguish than Rick Hill's, and a lot stringier, but also a lot more charming, since he's way more tongue-in-cheek.

The plot involves restoring Reena to the throne, for which they'll have to battle Amazons led by Maria Socas, as well as Sultana, an evil clone of Reena (Gabrielle again), and Jarek the evil wizard and Jimmy Fallon look-alike (John La Zar). Reena tells Deathstalker that if they succeed, he'll become a legend "right up there with Conan."

DS2 also casually references *Star Wars* (1977), the Bond flick *Goldfinger* (1964), and *The Pit and the Pendulum* (interestingly, the Vincent Price version from 1961 was also directed by Roger Corman). The whole thing is a virtuoso self-parody complete with cheesy outtakes in the closing credits, which are only marginally worse than what made it into the final cut.

Deathstalker III (a.k.a. Deathstalker and the Warriors from Hell) (1988) 🪓

Deathstalker III is so awful, not even *MST3K* can redeem it. Mr. Stalker (John Allen Nelson) here is less badass, more wiseass. The charm of *DS2* has been completely discarded. The sword-fighting scenes are just absurd. If you take a drink every time Deathstalker spins around in battle for no reason, you will wind up in the hospital. There's a peasant city raided, a lost princess looking for treasure, a useless wizard with an accent that is sometimes Scottish and sometimes Indian, and a magical object split in three that has to be made whole again (an idea later stolen by *Beastmaster 3*, although they probably all stole it from *Star Trek IV* [1986], which probably stole it from something else).

The villain's name is Troxartes (Thom Christopher), and he looks just like Ed Wood's chiropractor filling in for the late Bela Lugosi in *Plan 9 from Outer Space* (1959). Troxartes dresses like an extra from *Flashdance* (1983), minus the leg warmers. There is, arguably, one redeeming quality to this addition: A female friend of mine described this poofy-haired Deathstalker as "really hot." But she still left halfway through the movie. Let that be a lesson: It takes more than good looks to make a good barbarian film.

Deathstalker IV: Match of Titans (1991) 🪓🪓🪓

DS4 recycles Rick Hill and various clips from the other *Deathstalker* and *Barbarian Queen* flicks, not to mention the tournament-to-the-death plot of the first one, thus allowing entire scenes to be reused. The 'stalker (Hill) saves Dionara (Maria Ford) while again looking for his sword. He accompanies her to a tournament, and they work together as barbarian detectives to figure out why all the contestants are always drunk. It turns out that Kana (Michelle Moffett), the contest's hostess, is drugging the warriors so she can have her way with them (with more sinister motives I'll not reveal). "I need a man, the bigger, the better, and drunk!" Kana exclaims. Too bad she doesn't live near me

Along the way to the final rumble, there's a whole new mud-wrestling scene, some leather lesbo biker warriors, cat-people warriors of both genders, lots of drunks stumbling around, and, of course, pointless nudity. The plot highlight is Deathstalker teaching the virgin warrior Variat (Brett Baxter Clark) how to pick up girls so he can seduce Kana and figure out what's really going on.

DS4 is played a little more straight than *DS2* and *DS3*, which is OK, since at least Rick Hill looks the part of a warrior. Maria Ford is known for trying to actually *act* in the soft-core thrillers for which she's famous, and here she pulls it off, although she really didn't have to work so hard when surrounded by Hill and various dubbed Bulgarian supporting cast members.

And so, with *DS4*, the sun sets on the *Deathstalker* franchise (for now) with far more dignity than its rival series *Ator*, which strove so hard to be taken seriously and never even came close.

Fire and Ice (1983) ⚔⚔⚔⚔⚔⚔⚔

Produced by the winningly named Producers Sales Organization, this one's an animated film (rotoscoped, if you want to get picky) by barbarian cover king Frank Frazetta and counterculture exploitation king Ralph Bakshi. It was written by Gerry Conway and Roy Thomas, two writers for Marvel's *Conan* comics.

Led by the evil witch Juliana and her psychopathic wizard son Nekron, the kingdom of ice expands glacially southward using barking Neanderthals called Nekron Dogs as soldiers. When they run up against the fire kingdom, it's war. Caught between are Larn, a young barbarian warrior whose tribe gets wiped out, and Darkwolf, an unstoppable fighting machine in a cat mask who bears no small resemblance to Adam West. There's also Teegra, princess of the fire kingdom, who gets kidnapped by Nekron's henchmen but then escapes long enough to meet Larn. The fire team consists of redshirts who don't manage a kill anyone in the entire movie, except one scene where several inadvertently kill themselves. Along the way to the final conflict there are pterodactyls, giant water lizards, a troll, a witch, and a large bloodsucking centipede in a wide variety of landscapes (jungles, swamps, tundra, volcanoes, Mayan-style ruins, and so on). There's even a bit of pole vaulting.

Frazetta's influence shows in the exquisite design and color work, while Bakshi's surely responsible for the absurdly voluptuous princess, who spends almost the entire movie cavorting in an overstressed bikini top and microscopic purple thong that would be more at home in *Fritz the Cat*. There's a surprising lack of sex or gore (it's PG to *Heavy Metal*'s R), but it's quite an entertaining movie nonetheless. One could watch mainly for the artwork, but the movie exhibits dramatic merits as well. Between the lush landscapes, the mighty monsters, and the near-naked nymph, this is the perfect accompaniment for a teenage boy's first shrooming.

The only sad note is that Frazetta didn't execute background artist Thomas Kinkade once the movie wrapped. Kinkade's the guy whose glowing paintings of sugary cottages sweeten our shopping malls every holiday season, making all decent people want to puke. Thankfully, his work here is treacle-free.

Gor (1987) ⚔

Cannon Films brings us this outer-space sci-fi dreck loosely based on John Norman's novels. Tarl Cabot (Urbano Barbarini), a nerdy college professor, crashes his car and winds up on the planet Gor, located 180 degrees around the sun. There he becomes a hunk, fights barbarians, and frees slaves (temporarily) while trying to get home. It's pretty much the same as the "DEN" sequence from *Heavy Metal,* except it isn't funny and it expects to be taken halfway seriously. A last-minute appearance by Jack Palance sets up the dreadful sequel.

In the books, Gor frees Cabot to *enjoy* slaves. The Gorean "philosophy" is esoteric mumbo-jumbo with sex slaves as part of the natural order. It hasn't quite garnered the acceptance of L. Ron Hubbard's allegedly slave-loving money mill, Scientology, but it has a few practitioners nonetheless and seems harmless, if a little gormless. The movie has little to do with the philosophy, in any case.

Gunan, King of the Barbarians (a.k.a. The Invincible Barbarian) (1982) ⚔⚔⚔

Pietro Torrisi appeared in four barbarian movies in a two-year span (including a small part in *Ironmaster*), and this—well, this is one of them: a more-or-less quintessential example of the Italian barbarian cycle.

Bookended by narration about outer space and evolution (with dinosaur animations stolen from *One Million Years B.C.* [1966]), the movie really begins with the villain Nuriak (Emilio Messina) and his henchmen raiding the good guys' village and killing everyone. Gunan (Torrisi) and his twin brother are spirited away to the beach and found by Amazons in a sequence with lots of shots of people's feet.

The Amazons raise the twins and challenge them to see who's the invincible barbarian foretold in a prophecy. A series of slow-motion races and fights ensues. After Gunan's brother gets killed off (pretty much sealing the deal), Gunan prepares to fight the bad guys. He also falls in love with eyeliner-loving bombshell Lenni (Sabrina Siani in a nearly all-nude performance), who staggers out of the sea to reenact the famous kiss in *From Here to Eternity* (1953) with him.

GRÜTE SAYS

Sabrina Siani, why you no call Grüte back?

If you went to the beach with twenty hairy friends and a video camera, you could easily remake *Gunan* over a long weekend—but nobody would watch it without Siani in it.

Hawk the Slayer (1980) ⚔⚔⚔

This is a story of Heroic Deeds, the triumph of Good over Evil, and of a wondrous Sword wielded by a mighty Hero who appears when the Legions of Darkness stalk the land. That's what the opening titles say, anyway.

The movie falls between *Star Wars* (1977) and *Conan* (1982) chronologically, and the melancholy title hero (John Terry) combs his hair just like Han Solo and wears a studded blue vest. The wondrous sword in question, given to Hawk before the opening credits, is powered by a glowing nuclear rock known as "the last Elven Mindstone." Jack Palance gnaws black holes in the scenery as the villainous Voltan, who is apparently Hawk's brother despite a good thirty-year difference in their ages.

Hawk joins forces with another human warrior, an elf, a dwarf, and a giant (although the giant doesn't seem much bigger than Hawk) to fight Voltan and save a kidnapped abbess. Terry, better known these days for his work on *24* and *Lost*, lacks the roguish presence of any Deathstalker and seems kind of priggish. Then again, they're fighting to save a church.

This is a borderline barbarian movie, much more like a medieval spaghetti Western, minus spaghetti, with John Terry in the Eastwood role, flute trills on the soundtrack, and extreme close-ups. Hawk also wears a crucifix, which no decent Crom worshipper would ever do, but it turns out to have a spring-loaded knife built in, which I'm sure is just what Jesus had in mind.

Heavy Metal (1981) ⚔⚔⚔⚔⚔

Taking us back to a time when hard rock, nudity, drugs, and Dungeons & Dragons were the four horsemen of the anti-Reagan apocalypse, this is a set of loosely connected animated vignettes, about 50 percent barbarian and 50 percent sci-fi. It's well done and fun, and there are two barbarian segments, "Den" and "Taarna."

Den (John Candy) is a nerd teleported to another dimension, where he is transformed into a muscle-bound he-man. His first act is to fashion a crude loincloth: "There was no way

I was gonna walk around this place with my dork hanging out!" Then he has to save a girl and stop the bad guy from getting the Loc-Nar, a glowing green ball that is the source of all evil in the universe.

The "Taarna" part is bleaker. There's no actress to credit, since she doesn't have any spoken lines. Taarna flies around on a wide-eyed space ostrich and fights bad guys after her Taarakian people are wiped out. If my people are ever attacked by savage mutants, I hope our only protector won't spend forty-five minutes getting dressed up as a dominatrix. By the way, if you are somehow unaware of the magazine this movie derives from, become aware of it.

Heavy Metal 2000 (2000) ⚔⚔⚔

Julie Strain, an adult-film star, is lead voice actress *and* character model in this borderline sequel that straddles sci-fi and fantasy with only a pinch of barbarian. It continues the themes of the first movie, but the animation and art quality are subpar, the plot is pretty standard stop–the–evil magic, the music is monotonous, and there's none of the humor found in the predecessor. There's only one story, and it is essentially a rehash of the "Taarna" segment in the original. *HM2K*'s other grasping connections to its parent are a glowing green shard, lots of reptile-men getting slaughtered, and a drawn-out scene where the heroine, Julie, gets dressed for battle in a red vinyl bondage bikini thong thing. It's a watchable movie in its own right, but ultimately disappointing in light of the classic original. A more fitting follow up is supposedly in the works.

Hundra (1983) ⚔⚔⚔ ⚔⚔

"No man will ever penetrate my body with sword or himself," says the title heroine (Laurene Landon) in this ancestor to the *Kill Bill* films (2003, 2004). After her tribe of man-hating barbarians is wiped out by male barbarians who worship a bull, Hundra goes to get herself pregnant and replenish her tribe by using the seed of the same bad guys.

The opening sequence sets the bar with high-quality production and gorgeous photography that never—OK, *rarely*—betrays the film's low budget. *Hundra* doesn't become completely cheesy until halfway through, when Hundra gets to the city and befriends a peasant who sounds and looks like Mel Brooks. Meanwhile, the evil villain Nepakin (who is every bit as good-looking as the New York Dolls' David Johansen) and his dainty, closeted assistant scheme to capture Hundra.

If you look closely at the first barbarian leader (with the horned helmet) right before Hundra kills him, you'll notice Stars of David on his uniform, which I hope is unintentional. But there's also a theme of selective breeding here, given that Hundra doesn't want just any man's seed, only someone fit to the task. She's also a blue-eyed blonde. So Hundra is arguably a Nazi in addition to being a militant feminist, but she is nevertheless a total badass.

Highlights: Hundra's dog Beast, who she derides for being male, riding her horse. There's excellent stage combat in the opening and closing battles. The excessive screaming and yelling in combat scenes is hypnotic. While chewing on a rib, Hundra gets attacked and fights off her assailant while continuing to eat. She also spars with a rake-wielding midget who wears blue-and-red face paint like a New York Giants fan and then strips naked and rides her horse around in the sea.

If you only get to watch one barbarian movie besides *Conan the Barbarian* and *Beastmaster*, make it *Hundra*. And show it to your daughters, too. And if you don't have daughters, make some. As the closing voice-over tells us, "The seed of Hundra is in all women." Anyone who thinks *Red Sonja* is better has been brainwashed and should not be trusted.

Hundra's director, Matt Cimber, made another important contribution to barbarian culture, partnering with David McLane to create *Gorgeous Ladies of Wrestling* (*GLOW*) in the 1980s, which gave jobs to hundreds of barbarian women. He was also briefly married to Jayne Mansfield in the 1950s. Overall, a man of taste and refinement.

Ironmaster (1983) ⚔⚔⚔⚔

Spaghetti cannibal director Umberto Lenzi's *Ironmaster* opens with a caveman wandering around Custer, South Dakota, in a loincloth with an atrocious neckbeard, all set to a knockoff Ennio Morricone soundtrack by Guido and Maurizio de Angelis. A tribe of scruffy savages spy some plastic elephants and complain about having weak Stone Age weaponry. After a battle with a local tribe of ash-covered idiots, the tribe's resident bad guy Vood (played by George Eastman, a.k.a. Luigi Montefiori, a six-foot-nine Ringo Starr look-alike) kills the tribal elders and is exiled. Vood discovers iron ("a stone of divine power") after a volcanic eruption, kills some out-of-frame lions, joins up with a hottie named Lith (a Stone Age Lady MacBeth played by Pamela Prati), and starts the world's first arms race.

Vood, now unstoppable thanks to having one sword-shaped iron rod, takes over the tribe and militarizes them with dreams of conquest. He spends the rest of the movie wearing a dead lion's head. His rival is Ela, played by bodybuilder Sam Pasco—allegedly known in late-seventies gay circles as Mike Spanner, or "Big Max," a nude model/escort—in his first and only nonsmut appearance. Ela goes into exile and is promptly set upon by a pair of extremely fake-looking ape-men. He joins up with a nice blonde named Isa (Elvire Audray), who's done wonders with primitive Cover Girl and Aqua Net. They fight some ape-men, who, in a daring touch by Lenzi, have visible schlongs. While Vood conquers the nearby tribes, Ela joins a more civilized village of defenseless pacifists nearby and tries unsuccessfully to convince them to fortify their settlement against Vood. Vood inevitably enslaves the village, but Ela rallies and eventually triumphs when he invents a strategic weapon of his own.

A few memorable details: Throughout the film, characters refer to themselves in the third-person present tense, which does seem pretty barbaric (e.g., Ela says, "Wait, Ela goes with you."). In one scene, women struggle to turn a grindstone in a poor imitation of the famous scene from *Conan the Barbarian*. American National Enterprises, the original U.S. distributor, sounds like a great car-rental company.

Iron Warrior (a.k.a. Ator 3: Iron Warrior) (1986) ⚔⚔⚔

Alfonso Brescia's *Iron Warrior* is technically leaps and bounds beyond Joe D'Amato's *Ator* predecessors, with good lighting, better costumes, better acting, a quality score (including some *Miami Vice*–style bits), and full frontal nudity. But it's still Ator (Miles O'Keeffe), who is lifeless and stupid and lacking in charm (although O'Keeffe's so jacked that he doesn't really *need* charm). His only apparent motivation is booty of the female kind, which he pursues in a joyless, perfunctory way. You'd think an adventurer would show some actual zeal for adventuring. In fairness, *nobody* has any motivation in this movie, unless you count paychecks.

Ator sides with a good witch (Iris Peynado) and a princess (Savina Gersak) to battle the title warrior, Trogar (Franco Daddi) and Phoedra, the evil witch who controls him (Elisabeth Kaza). That's pretty much the entire plot, and most of the movie is just one challenge from the bad guys after another, without any rising action. Highlights are when Ator and Trogar take turns throwing spears at each other and catching them from the air. That's followed by a scene where the princess is dragged behind a horse for a while and then appears in the next scene without so much as a stain on her see-through dress. As in all good barbarian flicks, she also has a swimming scene. There are exploding boulders, magic spinning hula hoops, and weird magical space chicks—enough to earn *Iron Warrior* one ax more than its brethren.

Iron Warrior has some good short-term suspense, a sensible scarcity of dialogue, and above-average cinematography reminiscent of an art flick: lots of gauzy colored silk, and Ator waving his sword around on a cliffside. At the same time, the pacing is classic *Ator* (i.e., glacial) and the FX are pretty crap. Fog machines and an incessant use of the most amateur teleportation effect (pause filming, add/remove a character or object, resume filming) detract from a presentation that might otherwise look halfway decent.

Kull the Conqueror (1997) 🪓🪓🪓

Kull may predate Conan in the Robert E. Howard stories, but this movie is still a knockoff. Early on in the movie, the king of wherever (Sven Ole Thorsen) dies trying to kill Kull (Kevin Sorbo) and then gives Kull his crown with his dying breath. As the new king, Kull tries to modernize the place with a whole slew of American anachronisms like emancipating the slaves and granting religious freedom. The status quo doesn't like Kull's attitude and tries to kill him, but keeps screwing up, so they revive a three-thousand-year-old queen (Tia Carrera) with magic powers to do their dirty work. Kull unites with his psychic girlfriend Zareta (Karina Lombard) and a monk named Ascalante (G. Paul Davis) to set things right.

So, Kull's basically Abraham Lincoln with a battle-ax. You won't find too many modern viewers challenged by the pro-democracy message, even if it would have been anathema to Howard. (Lyon Sprague de Camp, the author who revived Conan after Howard's suicide and served as a technical adviser on this and the two *Conan* flicks, has often been criticized for "correcting" Howard's proto-Nazi eugenic tendencies.)

Overall, *Kull* isn't bad as a movie. It's well filmed and well scored (cheese-metal aside), and while the crawling hand of digital sorcery is evident, the effects don't ruin the movie. The acting is at least better than *Ator*'s, and Sorbo and Lombard make likable heroes. In an odd casting decision, Harvey Fierstein (who played a drag queen in *Torch Song Trilogy* [1988]) makes an appearance as a gravely voiced, merciless pirate. I don't want to spoil the ending, but the final fight sure reminded me of *Aliens* (1986). The highlight of the movie is when the old king's sniveling cousin gets thrown out a window, tumbles down a cliffside—and fucking *explodes*! The car-going-over-a-cliff trope is my favorite in all of movie-making, so this unique variant cements *Kull*'s third golden ax.

The Lustful Barbarian (a.k.a. The Long Swift Sword of Siegfried) (1971) 🪓🪓🪓

This is a soft-core porn version of *Die Niebelungen* complete with some sex scenes set to Wagner, with Siegfried played by Lance Boyle (a gross pseudonym for Raimund Harmstorf). A tangential barbarian movie at best, and something of a time capsule. The plot is straightforward: The title barbarian has sex with many different women. It features a young (though legal) Sybil Danning, who is also in *Warrior Queen* and *Amazon Women on the Moon*.

Masters of the Universe (1987) 🪓🪓🪓🪓

If your idea of a good time is to watch a gnome chauffeur He-Man, Duncan, and Teela around southern California in a pink Cadillac, then this is the movie for you! Dolph Lundgren is He-Man, battling against Frank Langella's Skeletor for control of Eternia in a movie derivative of *Star Wars* and *Conan* but with the strengths of neither. This was created while the *MoTU* cartoons were still on the air, so there's not a lot of exposition to clarify what's going on, but that's a good thing, since it would be gobbledygook anyway. Basically, there's a trippy "sonic key" that opens portals in the universe, and Skeletor wants it. He-Man and his friends accidentally transport the sonic key to present-day Earth, trailed by Skeletor's minions. A young couple (Courteney Cox and Robert Duncan McNeill) runs off with the sonic key, all hell breaks loose, and He-Man has to restore order.

The action sequences and effects in *Masters of the Universe* hold up OK, so why is this movie so tragically mediocre? Well, for one thing, Skeletor's henchmen learned marksmanship at the Imperial Stormtrooper Academy, so there's never much sense of danger. Much worse, the Eternian heroes learned acting from the action figures, leaving a pre-*Friends* Cox to do the emotional heavy lifting. But that's only part of the problem. I'd lay the heavy blame on Gwildor, the mangy, gnomish inventor played by the perpetually typecast Billy Barty. Gwildor's a cackling marketing gimmick who was added to the TV series and toy line after the movie. (Original sidekicks Orko and Battle Cat would have been too expensive for the production company, Cannon Films.)

Mattel deserves some blame, too, as they had final say over every aspect of the characters. As with Michael Bay's soul-crushing *Transformers* (2007) and its sequels, more crap movies nostalgically celebrating half-hour toy commercials, disappointment is inevitable to all but the most blinkered fans. A child's imagination is always going to come up with better plots than Hollywood hacks—like the time I crucified Orko, put my neighbor's Barbie in Hordak's Slime Pit, and fragged He-Man with an M-80.

The New Barbarians (1990) 🪓🪓
The New Barbarians 2 (1990) 🪓🪓🪓

People did have sex in the days of yore; otherwise none of us would be alive. And, yes, they enjoyed it, too. *The New Barbarians* teaches viewers about this aspect of history in unflinching graphic detail. In all honesty, this hard-core porno from the tail end of the hairy era has as much of a plot as *Ator*, and is much better lit. The costumes aren't bad, either, although they're only worn for brief moments. This movie also features one of the greatest barbarian hats you will ever see: It looks like a stuffed mechanical rodeo bull with Mr. Bill's face glued to it. There's a glowing green magical rock (Loc-Nar, anyone?) and, reaching out to its contemporaries *Beastmaster 2* and *Time Barbarians*, the movie's allegedly historical characters suddenly arrive in then-modern L.A. Kind of convenient, really, since that's where most porn is made.

The sequel picks up where its predecessor leaves off, when the characters who are lost in time return to their original barbarian era. Both movies are 79 minutes long, allowing for a truly epic double-feature pornographic fun-fest. (Although if you can watch 158 minutes of porn, you're probably doing something wrong.)

Red Sonja (1985) 🪓🪓🪓🪓

More watchable than *Conan the Destroyer* but no less tacky, this almost sequel features worse acting but better cinematography. Red Sonja (Brigitte Nielsen), thanks to her Asian trainers, is the greatest swordswoman in the world. Arnold Schwarzenegger plays Kalidor, a mysterious protector who fails to protect Sonja's sister, allowing the Loc-Nar (or, uh, some identical green glowing orb) to be taken away by the evil Queen Gedren (Sandahl Bergman). Kalidor is indistinguishable from Conan, prompting many to call this the third *Conan* movie, except here he just phones it in. After over an hour of assorted nonsense, Sonja, Kalidor, an annoying kid who knows kung fu, and the kid's slapstick bodyguard all storm Queen Gedren's papier-mâché castle, and hilarity ensues.

The Saga of the Viking Women and Their Voyage to the Waters of the Great Sea Serpent (1957) ⚔⚔⚔

Directed by Roger Corman. Black-and-white nudity-free starletsploitation. The Viking women, led by Desir (Abby Dalton), go to sea to rescue their lost, remarkably clean-shaven boyfriends. They piss off a rubber sea serpent and wind up enslaved by bad guys on an island. Meanwhile, Joel and the 'bots become obsessed with waffles—oh, sorry, that's just interstitial filler. But this is another movie that is simply unwatchable without *MST3K*.

She (1982) ⚔⚔⚔⚔⚔

If you've seen *She*, then you know it isn't strictly a barbarian film. However, it is titled *Barbarian* in some countries, it stars the lovely Sandahl "Valeria" Bergman dressed like a Corman Amazon, and, like nearly all barbarian movies, it opens with a peaceful village getting attacked by evil raiders. Also, it's totally fucking insane. It's a postnuclear film, but barbaric enough, set in "Year 23 after the Cancellation." She (Bergman) joins forces with another Amazon, named Shandra (Quinn Kessler) and two Deathstalker-type guys named Tom (David Gross) and Dick (Harrison Muller, Jr.) to find Hari (Elena Wiedermann), who has been kidnapped by the evil Norks.

This flick resists summary, but it includes Nazi footballers, telekinetic Communists, hedonistic vampire/werewolves, leprous mummies with chain saws, Bergman tied up and whipped, a Frankenstein monster in a box, a soundtrack joining Justin "Moody Blues" Hayward with Motörhead, a knockoff of Rod McKuen's "Soldiers Who Want to Be Heroes" on a mandolin, a bearded fat man in a pink tutu, and a guard named Xenon (David Traylor) who quotes movies in rapid-fire dialogue and can create clones from his own dismembered body (at one point, eight Xenons in sailor suits do a kickline down a bridge). It's like *The Warriors* (1979) marinated in *The Wiz* (1978) and served on a bed of *Conan,* forming a cinematic smorgasbord of all things great. There's a message in this Oz-like episodic adventure, but I'll be damned if I can figure out what it is. *She*'s key line is "Shandra, this has nothing to do with sense."

GRÜTE SAYS

What of fuck? She so crazy!

Sorceress (1982) ⚔⚔

New World Pictures brings us this old-world picture, apparently filmed before the invention of electric lighting, but with a staggering mastery of clichés. Two twin girls are mysteriously born several months old and given magical powers and fighting skills by Krona (Martin LaSalle), a good wizard who has just killed the evil wizard Traigon (Roberto Ballesteros). Traigon revives, looking about the same twenty years later and vows vengeance through confused arithmetic: "Find the two who are one!" I think there's also some magical object at stake, but ten minutes in, I'd already forgotten what it is.

The twin girls are apparently raised as boys, but we are reintroduced to them as adult women, doing what else but frolicking naked in a stream. There the two (helium-voiced

Playboy Playmates Lynette and Leigh Harris) expose their breasts and lack of other talent to a braying fawn named Pando (David Millbern). Meanwhile, their village is attacked by the villain's raiders, killing numerous extras. The twins join forces with a couple of male barbarians and Pando to fight Traigon and his faceless henchmen.

The rest is nearly unwatchable, even by Roger Corman standards (yes, he produced). The sound dubbing is hell, with the twins' voices coming off like Itchy and Scratchy from *The Simpsons*. In fairness, I saw a cruddy VHS transfer. No legal DVD version exists. But the technical quality's only part of the problem. The movie is so uninspired that it's not just forgettable; you can actually forget you're watching it *while you're watching it*.

If you have to watch any part of it, make it the last fifteen minutes, when there are explosions, marauding monkey-men and zombies, and a battle between a blue lion-bat-god thing and a face-god that shoots laser beams. There's also a light saber. The movie ends with the hint of an impending *ménage à trois*.

Do not confuse this with the 1995 film of the same name or its 2004 sequel, which feature *Heavy Metal 2000*'s Julie Strain in the flesh.

Super Stooges vs. the Wonder Women (a.k.a. Amazons vs. Supermen) (1975) ⚔⚔⚔

Another Alfonso Brescia *festa di formaggio*, this is a slapstick kung fu pic that pits three superheroes against a gang of idiotic thieves and a tribe of cruel, sexy Amazons. The "super stooges" of the title include a charlatan wizard who rules a valley and can jump very high (Aldo Canti, who was found shot in the head, presumably by the mob, outside Rome's Villa Borghese in 1991), an Asian martial arts expert (Hua Yueh), and a superstrong black man (Marc Hannibal, former Harlem Globetrotter and singer) who can knock people over by burping. The Amazons are trying to get access to the valley's Sacred Fire, which grants immortality to anyone who enters it. We quickly learn, though, that it's just a myth one of the supermen concocted to keep the peasants down. The super stooges join forces to protect the villagers from the Amazons.

The Amazons make the same cheer they made in Brescia's more serious *Battle of the Amazons*. There's a "nanny-nanny-boo-boo" horn riff repeated whenever a villain gets abused, on top of the already goofy Moog music. It's all pretty dumb, but as a mash-up of barbarianism, superhero movies, and kung fu, it actually sort of works: It's well paced and inventive and has enough "You gotta be kidding me" moments to keep you watching. At the very least, *Stooges* should be a stoner classic.

The Sword and the Sorcerer (1982) ⚔⚔⚔

Lee Horsley plays Talon, a roguish warrior, in this competent and relatively complex sword-and-sorcery flick. It's a revenge plot, with a princess and an evil king named Cromwell (not to be confused with Britain's Lord Protector, Charles I's nemesis), but there's also a more interesting bad guy: Richard Moll (Bull from the 1984–1992 sitcom *Night Court*), the toxic avenger and titular sorcerer who may be the most malevolent and best-costumed villain in this list. The most memorable element here is Talon's triple-pronged Sly Sword, which, uh, shoots swords. (*Awesome!!!*) There's a lot of low lighting and soft focus, and nifty purple sparks when swords connect in the sword fights.

This isn't really a barbarian movie, but with lines like "I can't wait to bed you, wench," it comes close enough, and one of the characters is referred to as a barbarian. Fun fact: This flick outdid *Conan the Barbarian* at the box office in 1982 and was the biggest indie hit of the year. The trailer, clearly pandering to the zeitgeist, advertised both dungeons and dragons. There is a dungeon but no dragon—just ornate fog machines. This movie used enough fog machines for a lifetime of Spinal Tap concerts.

The credits hint at a sequel called *Tales of an Ancient Empire*, which director Albert Pyun actually made twenty-eight years later. According to Pyun, he and the producers didn't do the sequel earlier, because *The Sword and the Sorcerer* made so much money, they never had to work again. Unfortunately, they did (see the review of *Tales of an Ancient Empire* below).

Sword of the Barbarians
(a.k.a. Barbarian Master) (1982) ⚔

Michele Massimo Tarantini's flick opens with a village getting attacked. The hero's traveling companions are a girl and an Asian guy. Sadly, though, *Conan* this is not. Sangraal (Pietro Torrisi), the head of a tribe of mangy peasants, leads his people in search of new lands and a seven-foot-long crossbow (instead of the usual sword). It's the standard fare of the hero looking for some mystical thing to get revenge (in this case for his murdered wife) and surviving numerous mini-quests and half-assed attempts at drama.

Highlights include a villain's hat designed to look like a steel duck with outstretched wings and a scene where the leads splash around in a creek, pretending to struggle, and then fall off a five-foot waterfall. Most notable is the mystical scene where the always luscious Sabrina Siani descends from the clouds in an orgy of glitter, claws Sangraal with sharpened press-on nails, and sashays back into oblivion.

Tales of an Ancient Empire (2010) ⚔⚔

Pros: some decent cinematography, lots of attractive people, passable costumes, brief nudity, gore, decent fake vampire teeth, and the return of the Sly Sword. Cons: everything else! It's totally unwatchable, frustrating, confusing, and butchered by a spastic editor. It gives us incessant "What do you seek, wanderer?"–type dialogue, laughable CGI, eight minutes or so of expository opening credits (with bad grammar and typos: "Different mothers, but sired the same father"), then constant spoken exposition (as opposed to anything actually happening onscreen), an artificial "tales" framework, *entire scenes that seem to be missing*, inaudible line readings (particularly from the vampires, slurring with their false teeth), and a mix of horrible hard rock and heavy-handed orchestral music. Oh, and it has fifteen minutes of closing credits!

Director Albert Pyun claims the opening is being redone, and the sequel, *Red Moon*, will apparently resolve the plot, whatever the plot is. It manages to make *Ator* flicks seem coherent. I give it one grudging star for the efforts of Kevin Sorbo and Lee Horsley, the only actors with a pulse in this fiasco.

Tarkan and the Blood of the Vikings
(a.k.a. Tarkan Versus the Vikings) (1971) ⚔⚔⚔⚔⚔

Tarkan is one of a handful of memorable movies from Turkey's golden age of schlocky action movies, to which we also owe *Altar* (1985), *Dünyayı Kurtaran Adam* (1982), and *Turist Ömer Uzay Yolunda* (1973) (the Turkish *Conan*, *Star Wars*, and *Star Trek*, respectively). Unlike the others, though, *Tarkan* is at least as original as its source, Sezgin Burak's popular comic book series.

Somehow raised by wolves to be a master swordsman, the Hunnic hero Tarkan (Kartal Tibet) travels with only his wolf "brother" Kurt and Kurt's son, who is also named Kurt. In an interesting take on history, the Vikings have allied with the Chinese to fight the Huns. In the opening fight, the elder Kurt gets killed off by the evil Viking general Tora (Bilal Inci), begetting the plot in which Tarkan and his wolf both tearfully vow revenge. Despite the Turkish boasts about their fighting prowess—"We have three squadrons of Turkish women here, each worth ten men!" a Hun explains—the Vikings and Chinese capture the female Huns and kill everyone else. Luckily, Attila is away on a campaign, because otherwise he would be *pissed*.

The Vikings sacrifice enemies by tying them to a dock so they can be eaten by a giant inflatable octopus. After leading a coup, Tora uses this rather convoluted method of execution to dispose of the Viking king and his daughter Ursula (Eva Bender). Ursula survives, though, to lead a group of good Viking Valkyries in pink-and-turquoise-shag tunics who are accompanied by a grunting half-witted giant named Orso (Hüseyin Alp), who was separated at birth from Richard Kiel. Ursula ultimately unites with Tarkan (in both senses) to destroy the evil Vikings, restore her dynasty to power, kill the mega-octopus, crush the Chinese, and rescue the captured Hunlets.

This is a brightly colored gem of a movie. Zealous editing ensures there's never a scene with nothing happening. It's packed with fast-paced, ridiculous fights, including one where Orso fights off a group of men using a dinner table and another where Tarkan somehow defends himself against four mind-bogglingly stupid swordsmen while his wrists are tied to a log. The Vikings are also shockingly incapable of hurting Kurt. Even when tied up, he manages to bite Toro and defend himself unscathed against twelve hesitant Vikings with long spears.

All the costumes appear to be made from carpet samples, and many of the Vikings wear wigs the color of Tang and fake handlebar mustaches ready to fall off at any moment. There's plenty of gory violence, a solid dosage of sex, and a few combinations of the two. There are also more blatantly intentional up-skirt shots than in even the mighty *Hundra*, thanks to the micromini tunics worn by both men and women. Other highlights: Kurt fighting the octopus, several bloody-ax-in-the-head shots, Kurt sitting still and panting or wandering off-camera while Tarkan's attacked, a pointless but awesome strip dance by the Chinese princess Lotus while Tarkan dangles over a pit of snakes, and an orgiastic feast that culminates in a Hun girl tortured *on a trampoline*. *Tarkan and the Blood of the Vikings* sets the bar very high, and should not be missed.

The 2004 Mondo Macabro edition features an interesting documentary about the rise and fall of this period of Turkish cinema in general. To my knowledge, the other six *Tarkan* movies (four of which star Tibet) are not available in English.

GRÜTE SAYS

Tarkan have awesome mustache!

Thor the Conqueror (1983) ⚔

Swelling, Wagnerian orchestral music launches us into Tonino Ricci's *Thor the Conqueror*, with the camera lingering on a dark hill where absolutely nothing is happening for a good minute. The opening voice-over (all the Italian barbarian flicks have one) is from the sorcerer Etna (Christopher Holm), who raises Thor (Bruno Minniti). Etna's magic power is to turn into an owl. In an unusual and pointless moment, he addresses the audience directly in the manner of a Shakespeareian soliloquist while Thor is present: "I have taught Thor combat . . ." Shortly thereafter, he announces resignedly, "All I eat is fish heads, take no offense. I must face it, it is my time to depart. Time to die." Etna doesn't die, though. Instead, he follows Thor slavishly and calls out instructions to him so that Thor, who might otherwise do nothing, will do *something*.

In the movie's most laughable moment, Thor is taunted by motionless drawings of laughing zombie clowns projected on a cave wall. And then there's Etna's best line, explaining a mysterious equine creature to Thor: "Centuries from now, it will be called a horse." If I didn't know better, I'd think Thor was a masterful parody. It is so ridiculous it manages to achieve the sought-after status of "So bad it's good."

The Throne of Fire (1983) ⚔⚔⚔

Pietro Torrisi and Sabrina Siani unite under the aegis of director Franco Prosperi once again to bring us this plodding cheesefest that's marginally better than *Gunan* only because Siani gets more screen time. Siegfried (Torrisi) once again descends from Wagnerian heights to act in a cheap Italian movie where he must marry Princess Valkari (Siani), fight Belial's evil messenger Morak (played by Harrison Muller, also of *She*), and gain control of the throne of fire (which is a literal name; it shoots flames).

Even in Italy, this Franco Prosperi is often confused with the Franco Prosperi who directed *Mondo Cane* (1962) and subsequent exploitation documentaries. Which Prosperi is more talented? Let the debate begin.

Time Barbarians (1990) ⚔

The plot of *Time Barbarians* is basically the same as *Beastmaster 2*, but this film lacks comedy, drama, special effects, or anything interesting whatsoever. It's not even so-bad-it's-good, which usually requires the director to have some warped vision. The actors seem to be doing their best, so I won't criticize them, given that the script is stultifying and the editing is nonexistent. Nearly all of the film's hacking and slashing occurs out of frame, presumably to avoid expensive blood effects. The writer/director pies himself in the face just seconds into the movie, with the scrolling titles that begin "In an ancient time of swords and scorcery [sic] . . . " Only the topless scenes (or all the scenes with the lead barbarian, Deron "Malibu" McBee, strutting around, if that's your thing) elevate this incoherent messterpiece to one star.

The Warrior and the Sorceress (1984) ⚔⚔⚔⚔

If you've seen the samurai flick *Yojimbo* (1961), or the Western *A Fistful of Dollars* (1964) (or the dozen other variations), you're already familiar with the plot of this barbarians-on-another-planet movie. David Carradine, as the warrior Kain, shows up in a town and manipulates two opposing warlords into fighting each other. Here the central object of dispute is a well. Carradine's moppy gray hair, puckered-lip scowls, and slouching stride hardly prove him a substitute for Toshirô Mifune or Clint Eastwood. But in the older films, you don't get a princess who's topless in every scene, slimy tentacled reptile puppets, or a stripper with four boobs. The so-called sorceress Naja (Maria Socas) never really does anything to earn that job title other than watch someone forge a magic sword.

Socas also played the Amazon Queen in *Deathstalker 2*. And Anthony de Longis, here one bad guy's lieutenant, was Blade in *Masters of the Universe* and Morthond in *Circle of Iron* (also with Carradine). All of which goes to show you that once you're in the barbarian movie world, there is no escape.

Yor, the Hunter from the Future (1983) ⚔⚔⚔⚔

Supposedly, 40 percent of Americans believe that dinosaurs and humans lived at the same time. Some blame *The Flintstones*, but I blame *Yor*. After a New Wave opening song, "Yor's

World—He's the Man," the movie finds its eponymous hero (Reb Brown)—who looks just like Jeff Spicoli from *Fast Times at Ridgemont High* (1982)—battling a triceratops and then drinking its blood. Not long after, Yor is thrown a few hundred feet off a cliff and survives without a scratch. This experience somehow prompts him to shoot a giant bat and use its corpse as a hang glider.

The premise of the movie is that Yor is searching for his roots, symbolized by the peculiar gold disco medallion he wears. But he spends the first sixty minutes just wandering around killing everyone he meets and pissing off his possessive girlfriend Ka-Laa (Corinne Cléry). *Yor* is a mash-up of different genres and not entirely barbarian, but it's a rather inventive flick. Without spoiling what a generous person would call the "plot," there is a reason Yor is "from the future."

As a footnote, Brown went on to become chief operating officer of Sierra Entertainment, the company that made the King's Quest games.

— ALSO NOTABLE —

Altar (1985)
Often referred to as the "Turkish *Conan*." Good luck finding it in English.

The Archer: Fugitive from the Empire (1981)
A TV movie that's now impossible to find, about an archer who is a fugitive from the empire.

Army of Darkness (1992)
Ash from the *Evil Dead* movies gets thrown back in time with a chain saw stuck to his hand. An endlessly quotable movie that basically godfathered the video game *Doom* (1993).

Barbarian Days (2011)
A documentary about the Robert E. Howard Celebration, which takes place every June at the Robert E. Howard Museum in Cross Plains, Texas.

Barbariana: Queen of the Savages (2009)
An amateur spoof that's still better than *Wizards of the Demon Sword*. I liked the barbarian-on-the-throne scene at the end, an homage to the last scene of *Conan* (which was itself derived from Frank Frazetta). Epileptics should be cautious, though. *Barbariana*'s available in five parts on YouTube.

GRÜTE SAYS

Stay away from my MeTube, evil witch!

Beowulf (2007)

The epic hero, played by Ray Winstone, battles to kill Crispin Glover and Angelina Jolie, or at least their voices, as it's all CGI.

GRÜTE SAYS

CGI make Grüte puke in popcorn!

Burebista (1980)

A Romanian movie about real-life Romanian barbarians.

Cannibal Women in the Avocado Jungle of Death (1989)

Shannon Tweed and Bill Maher hunt Adrienne Barbeau in this Amazon-comedy version of *Heart of Darkness*.

Colossus and the Huns (a.k.a. Tharus figlio di Attila) (1962)

One of a billion sword-and-sandal cheapies from the sixties, this one happens to involve the Huns.

Conan the Barbarian (2011)

Jason Momoa takes over for Arnold Schwarzenegger in this twenty-first-century Hollywood reboot.

The Devil's Sword (1984)

Totally awesome Indonesian martial arts flick where Barry Prima battles the Crocodile Queen over a magical sword that can rule the world. Everyone gets decapitated.

Eyes of the Serpent (a.k.a. In the Time of the Barbarians 2) (1994)

Good sister (wearing brown leather) fights evil sister (wearing black leather) to see who is more clichéd.

Goliath and the Barbarians (1959)

Steve Reeves fights barbarians in the fourth century BCE.

Hercules in New York (1970)

Not exactly a barbarian film, since Hercules isn't a barbarian, although he has prodigious strength and wears animal skins. But really isn't anything with Arnold Schwarzenegger sort of barbaric? There are, of course, a billion Hercules movies.

The Norseman (1978)

Lee Majors plays a Viking searching for his father, who has been kidnapped by Native Americans.

Nymphoid Barbarian in Dinosaur Hell (1990)

A Troma flick with a bikini barbarian fighting mutants and reptile people.

Outlaw of Gor (1989)

The sequel to *Gor*, or, as it might be better known, a late *MST3K* episode.

Pathfinder (2007)

Vikings maraud a Native American village and accidentally leave behind one of their kids, who grows up to be a fierce warrior who slaughters Vikings.

Phoenix the Warrior (a.k.a. She-Wolves of the Wasteland) (1988)

Postnuke biker barbarian chicks battle it out for who gets the last man on Earth in a festival of Velveeta-grade acting.

Prehistoric Women (a.k.a. Slave Girls) (1967)

Adventurers kidnapped by bikini-wearing blonde Amazons are forced to have sex with the queen, Martine Beswick, on the set of *One Million Years B.C.*

Ronal the Barbarian (2011)

A Danish CGI parody of barbarian movies, featuring the voices of Brigitte Nielsen and Sven Ole Thorsen.

Rusichi (a.k.a. Kampf der Barbaren) (2008)

The German title of this Russian film translates to *Battle of the Barbarians*. Unfortunately, this film exists only in those languages. It is nicely filmed, and the battle scenes are very good. Hopefully, someone will bring this to the United States.

The Seven Magnificent Gladiators (1983)

An attempt to cross *Conan the Barbarian* and *The Magnificent Seven* (1960), with Lou Ferrigno and Sybil Danning at the center. Celebrated for its magnificent catfight.

Sheena: Queen of the Jungle (1984)

Tanya Roberts does a Tarzan impression.

Stormquest (1987)

Jungle Amazons led by a sexy shemale.

UHF (1989)

I can't call this a barbarian movie in any real sense, but you do get the thirty-second spoof trailer for the much-anticipated *Conan the Librarian*.

The Viking Queen (1967)

Very loosely based on the story of Boudica.

Warrior Queen (1987)

Sybil Danning, among others, going soft-core in Pompeii. Rick "Original Deathstalker" Hill's in this, too.

Warrior Queen (a.k.a. Boudica) (2003)

Boudica of the Iceni battles the Romans. Besides the other *Warrior Queen* reviewed above, there was also a British *Warrior Queen* series about Boudica made in 1978.

Wizards of the Demon Sword (1991)

Trash cinema from the masters at Troma, with director Fred Olin Ray ably wasting the talents of Laurence Tierney and Michael Berryman, who must have needed a quick buck.

Wizards of the Lost Kingdom (1985)

Youth-oriented cheapo Corman schlock about a magical boy and his albino Chewbacca clone, Gulfax, searching for a magic ring, with reams of reused footage from *Deathstalker* and *Sorceress*.

GRÜTE SAYS

Deathstalker me favorite documammary!

Wizards of the Lost Kingdom 2 (1989)

There's something terrifyingly awesome about filming a pile of shit and releasing it to universal disdain, then turning around and making a sequel. But who cares, when you can make a movie that just recycles footage from *The Warrior and the Sorceress* and *Barbarian Queen*?

APPENDIX D
How to Make a Barbarian Movie

A barbarian village gains a new slave girl.
Somewhere else, a kingdom has lost a princess.

—Tad de Neeve, *writer/director/producer of the films* Babor the Derivative
(1983), Bor, the Deathseeking Osprey of Mightiness (1985), Bor II: Bor and the
Magic Thing (1992), Bor 3: Bor vs. the Actors from Troll 2 (1994), Cimmerian
She-Sluts (1995), *and* Bor in the Land of the Leather Bondage Queen (1999)

[Barbarian movies] are . . . cheap.

—*Marshall McLuhan*

The barbarian genre is formulaic, but the formula is necessary. When the barbarian stands alone on a mountaintop and beseeches his gods, the gods respond by sending wave after wave of faceless henchmen. They are nothing but pointless obstacles, but they are sent to teach the barbarian to trust only his sword and his strength. And the actual goal is always a doomed physical romance and a magic jewel with a green LED in it. Since the lead barbarian is always aware of the foolishness of his effort, the philosophical message is clear: Life is meaningless.

Somebody has to produce these movies and spread this barbaric message. And there's a major upside to being that person. What other type of film has the power to amuse, amaze, and arouse, all on a budget under two hundred bucks?

PREPRODUCTION

Get Actors

When making a barbarian movie, you can hire the actors before you write the script. If Arnold Schwarzenegger and Marc Singer are busy, you will need a bunch of Italians and a lot of olive oil (they may supply their own). You will also need a large-breasted female, or preferably several. For your villain, any hard-

on-his-luck middle-aged man with a stentorian voice will do. You can find individuals who meet these criteria outside bus stations. Often, they don't even need costumes. (In fact, homeless people make great peasant extras and will work for peanuts, literally.) If you really want to mix things up, a large-breasted female can also work as your villainess, but this may strain your budget, since black leather bustiers with embroidered bat wings do not come cheap. A male villain should look like the drummer from Spinal Tap or should be played by Rip Torn.

You will also need one Asian cast member to play the martial arts expert. You can use a Latino if you are able to tape his eyes into a squint, but he has to look Asiatic. Having an Asian in your movie lends it more historical legitimacy, dramatically increasing your odds of getting an Oscar nod.

Scripting

First, you'll need a story. This part is extremely easy. Let's start by naming your character. First, choose a prefix and a suffix from the table below.

DETERMINING YOUR BARBARIAN'S FIRST NAME

Prefix	Suffix	Prefix	Suffix
Arn-	-an	Mo-	-gör
Aster-	-andy	Nän-	-hold
Bäb-	-anth	Obel-	-itsy
Cön-	-ar	Pa-	-ix
D-	-arth	Räy-	-k
Fay-	-äx (or -äxe)	Rhein-	-ki
Gr-	-bär	Schnä-	-ll
Häg-	-bard	Ste-	-oö
Hö-	-därr (or -där)	Sun-	-pu
Ku-	-dö	Thrö-	-tt
Lum-	-gö	Thun-	-ud

Next, give your character a title from the table below. This title will be integrated intö yöur prötägonist's name like so: [Prefix][Suffix] the [Title], ör the variatiön [Prefix][Suffix], the [Title] (the sepärating comma is really impörtant to certain barbarians).

Söme famous examplës: Häwk the Släyer and Atör, the Fighting Eagle.

DETERMINING THE REST OF YOUR BARBARIAN'S NAME

Barbarian	Fearless	Skullcrusher
Uncivilized	Fist	Needler
Primal	Unimpeachable	Nagger
Wanderer	Mighty	*...continued on next page*

Obliterator	Giant-Shortener	Vigorous
Destroyer	Infester	Contemptible
Cruiser	Fighting Eagle	Penetrator
Aircraft Carrier	Eviscerator	Refrigerator
Impaler	Backscratcher	Indefatigable
Horrible	Eye Irritant	Liver-Extractor
Conqueror	Competent	Hunter from the Future
Muscular	Hurtful	Defenestrator
Bonesmasher	Tasty	Cranial Melon-Baller
Scalper	Merciless	Unsinkable
Slayer	Rarely, but Occasionally,	Hoople
Scratcher	Merciful	Mok
Frustrating	Alcoholic Yak	

Next, decide on your hero's backstory. You can get really involved with this, but we recommend that you follow the simple directions below.

Your barbarian character is born in (choose one)
- ☐ the basement of the king's palace, from which he is smuggled to a squalid peasant village.
- ☐ a squalid peasant village, from which he is smuggled to the basement of the king's palace.
- ☐ a hut somewhere not far from a major city ruled by an evil wizard.
- ☐ a remote, defenseless village where peasants are always raking leaves for some reason.
- ☐ a trailer in Nevada.

He is born with (choose one or more)
- ☐ a magic amulet.
- ☐ a magic sword.
- ☐ a spear and a magic helmet.
- ☐ a really big sword with a mysterious engraving.
- ☐ the magic power to speak to animals.
- ☐ the magic power to make lip movements that correspond to Italian pronunciations while actually speaking English.

Now that you've established your character's background, you can move on to the story proper, which will involve some kind of love interest justifying snippets of female nudity and episodes of poorly choreographed medieval combat. During the course of your movie, the following should occur:

Your hero finds his girlfriend (choose one)

- ☐ in a lake.
- ☐ in a pond.
- ☐ in a river.
- ☐ in a dungeon.
- ☐ when he pillages a town and rapes everyone in it but her.
- ☐ online, in World of Warcraft.
- ☐ at a comic book convention, dressed as Catwoman.

She is a princess who has been enslaved and is scantily clad. Her personality can be characterized as (choose any or all)

☐ sassy.	☐ sultry.	☐ spunky.
☐ snippy.	☐ slutty.	☐ skanky.
☐ snotty.	☐ slinky.	

Wearing a miniskirt, your barbarian must gather a band of quarrelsome helpers to defeat an evil wizard and (choose one)

- ☐ save the princess.
- ☐ learn the true meaning of love.
- ☐ travel through time to prevent the Kennedy assassination.
- ☐ teach some high school geeks how to get girls.

Other than the ubiquitous girlfriend, his quarrelsome helpers include (select any)

- ☐ an annoying twelve-year-old with magic powers.
- ☐ an old, bald martial arts expert from the Orient who speaks in riddles.
- ☐ a dog who is always hungry.
- ☐ a wise and magical black man.
- ☐ a Turk with a scimitar.

- ▢ the last survivor from some race of dumb warriors that encourages martyrdom and got wiped out.
- ▢ an inarticulate giant with an ax.
- ▢ a cockatoo named Spike.
- ▢ a wise-talking peasant with a Brooklyn accent.
- ▢ a paranoid android.
- ▢ the girlfriend's nagging mother.
- ▢ a magical flying vacuum cleaner in a cloak.
- ▢ some rabid ferrets.

A barbarian never passes up a battle, no matter how suicidally mismatched and avoidable it may be. So, along the way, he must have seemingly pointless fights with groups of (choose as many as you like)

- ▢ hairy cavemen.
- ▢ dinosaurs.
- ▢ cavemen riding dinosaurs.
- ▢ dinosaurs riding cavemen.
- ▢ brainwashed peasants.
- ▢ robots in chain mail.
- ▢ bats.
- ▢ stuntmen in bear suits.
- ▢ superintelligent Arctic wolves.
- ▢ pygmies.
- ▢ sand people.
- ▢ mummy sand people.
- ▢ mole people.
- ▢ cat people.
- ▢ Italians.

The evil wizard knows what the barbarian is doing at all times, thanks to (choose one)

- ▢ telekinesis.
- ▢ a crystal ball.
- ▢ an oily bird of prey that serves as a spy, or a robotic version of same, or flying monkeys.
- ▢ a double agent among the barbarian's helpers.
- ▢ a bubbling cauldron that inexplicably shows it all.
- ▢ strategically placed CCTV cameras.
- ▢ having read the script before filming commenced.

In the climactic battle, the evil wizard (choose one)

- ▢ grabs the barbarian and stuffs him in a cage.
- ▢ grabs the princess and stuffs her in a cage.

O captures the barbarian's friends and puts them in a cage.

O accidentally puts himself in the cage.

O grabs the princess and threatens her with a steak knife or some magical green-glowing jewel made of plastic.

To add a sense of the unexpected to this climactic battle
(choose one, two, or many)

O the barbarian's friends escape their captors and show up at just the right moment and save him.

O the barbarian uses some reflective object to make the evil wizard's magic spell turn against him.

O the barbarian fights his way to the wizard and throws him into a pool of fire, lava, or olive oil.

O the magic object that everyone forgot about somehow saves the barbarian's life.

O a bunch of random henchmen die from being punched in the face.

O something catches fire, escalating the tension.

O orchestral horn music plays on the soundtrack, escalating the tension.

O the evil wizard becomes afraid, runs away, and falls out a window.

Finally (choose one)

O the wizard dies and there's a magical explosion and the barbarian frees the princess and kisses her.

O the barbarian dies and the studio goes out of business, but the movie becomes a hit in Sweden.

O the barbarian flees, abandoning his friends, and lives out his life in shame on the professional-wrestling circuit.

O one of the quarrelsome helpers makes a really bad joke, there's a freeze frame, and a title card with the words "The End . . . or is it?" comes on screen.

There are some other general rules that you should take into account as you are working out the details of your plot, if it is to be properly set in the primitive world of barbarian adventure:

- Anything made of glass is magical.
- Science is evil.
- Machines are bad.

PRODUCTION

Financing

Now that you have a script, you will need to secure financing. To get investors, be sure to give your production company an appealing name like Leisure Investment Company. A recommended budget is about two hundred dollars. If you can't scrape that together, you can still turn your script into a comic book and hand it out to strangers on the subway.

Costuming

Costuming is perhaps the easiest part of the whole process, since you really only need to stitch together some old kitchen rags to make a loincloth. And here's a tip: Wrap some belts around the hero's pecs. It will make them more pronounced and draw attention away from other parts of his costume that may be lacking. Run over some squirrels or rabbits and tie their carcasses together for the other costumes. For the female lead and her friends, more loincloths are in order. To make a barbarian bra, buy a large stew ladle, cut off the handle and cut the cup in half. Rivet it to a couple of leather belts. There you have it—instant metal bikini top. Another option is to use some colorful bar mitzvah yarmulkes. If you steal them from any nearby synagogue, you can be reasonably sure that there will be a couple of gold- or silver-colored ones.

Filming

Filming should only take a day. Wake up early and spend the morning listening to Quiet Riot and eating psychedelic mushrooms with your actors. Now sneak onto a farm and punch all the animals. Film everything that happens. For lighting, just use tiki torches, which are available in the barbecue section of your nearest Walmart. Be careful, though. If any actual barbarians see you filming, they may mistake you for food.

POSTPRODUCTION

Music

Horns plus timpani for any galloping-on-horseback and swordplay scenes. Swelling strings for the love scenes or any time the hero looks wistfully to the horizon and talks about his mother. A glockenspiel (or a triangle) adds a mechanical sound for any scenes in cities or where the characters make swords. All these can be added in via simple MIDI keyboard. Or you can just steal the music from some other barbarian movie.

Editing

Whatever you filmed can simply be slapped together. Nobody said this movie has to be coherent. Although, if your film makes no sense at all, you can always retitle it as a postnuclear-fallout movie. If your movie doesn't quite hit the sweet spot (70–100 minutes), pad it out with montages of the barbarian waving his sword around on a mountainside, or B-roll shots of peasants raking leaves and squinting at the sun.

Legal

You'll discover that your movie is identical to one of the Barbarian Boom flicks created in the early 1980s, most likely by Cannon Films. Don't worry: Blatant plagiarism never stopped anyone from making a barbarian movie. In fact, quite a few barbarian movies use scenes from other movies, with or without permission. If in doubt, have your lead actor stand around waving his broadsword on a cliff top in the glow of your planet's twin shining suns. Might will win the day over litigiousness, as it always should. The enemy lawyers will wet their pants and flee.

Distribution

Direct-to-video, or YouTube. If you go with video, remember to put the hero on the cover with his woman clutching his calves. And you can never have too many skulls.

Marketing

This takes care of itself. Men will come for the leather bustiers, and women will watch for the tan, muscle-bound heroes dripping with grease.

The Premiere

Should have lots of drugs and strippers to distract people from the movie, and should devolve into an orgy.

Dr. Byron Clavicle (seated) and Grüte Skullbasher

Acknowledgments

Special thanks to John Burns for his practical assistance, Brian Orban for his endless knowledge, the Gerli brothers for their undying wisdom, the gentleman and lady of the Portland Accord art collective for their baffled encouragement, and Teddie Goldenberg IV for introducing me to Conan way back in the Dark Ages. Further thanks to the thousands of creative people in film, TV, and comics, and one particular suicidal Texan writer, all of whose work I have tried to honor in these pages as barbarically as possible (i.e., by pillaging it).

Dr. Byron Clavicle

GRÜTE SAYS

You buy book? Me not burn your village.

Contributors

DR. BYRON CLAVICLE is the acclaimed author of over four thousand works of academic scholarship in the field of barbarian studies, having published articles in periodicals such as *Field and Stream* and *Vogue*, as well as several letters to *Penthouse*. His recent books include *Crushing Your Enemies for Fun and Profit* and *Everything You Ever Wanted to Know about Yaks (But Were Afraid to Ask)*. He is hard at work on a first novel, *Latex Sluts vs. Zombie Frankenstein*.

GRÜTE SKULLBASHER is a Bunglorian barbarian king and the dean of discipline at Princeton University. When not leading his deadly armies in the merciless slaughter of opposing hordes, he enjoys eating food and having sex. He was also a technical consultant for *American Gladiators*. Visit Grüte at www.skullbasher.com.

BENJAMIN CHADWICK is a writer who lives in North America.

JOSHUA KEMBLE is an award-winning illustrator who lives in Long Beach, California, with his wife, Mai Kemble, and pugs. His work can be viewed at www.joshuakemble.com.

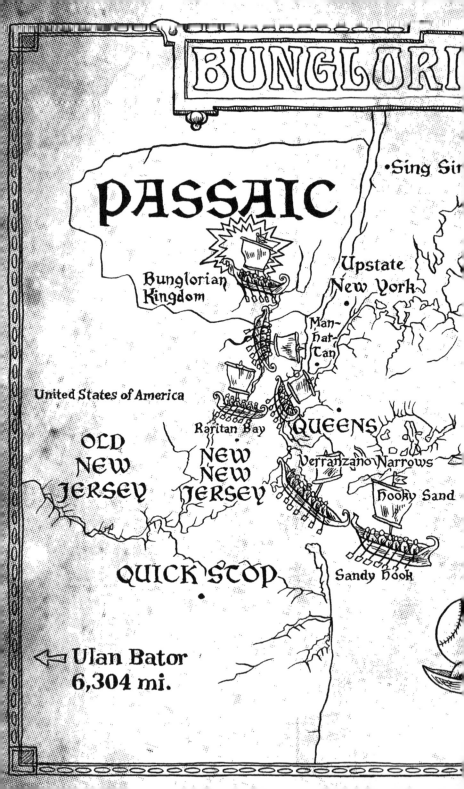